NOURISHING SOCIAL RENEWAL

for Rupert

from

Dick

NOURISHING SOCIAL RENEWAL

by teaching people how to
feed each others needs

Dr Dick Atkinson OBE

BREWIN BOOKS

First published by
Brewin Books Ltd, 56 Alcester Road,
Studley, Warwickshire B80 7LG in 2012
www.brewinbooks.com

ISBN: 978-1-85858-492-8

A Cataloguing in Publication Record
for this title is available from the British Library.

Typeset in New Baskerville
Printed in Great Britain by
TJ International Ltd.

CONTENTS

ACKNOWLEDGEMENTS

This book is not based on some theory or political ideology. So, it need pay no tribute to any party or to political philosophies of this or that bent. Rather, it is based on the hard practical work and determination of a host of people living and working in Balsall Heath, which was once Birmingham's least desirable neighbourhood and is now one of its most attractive ones. There are so many people to mention that it is not possible except in general terms. Thanks are due to most residents, several thousands of them. But, these stand out:

Ted Wright	Raja Amin	Naseem Akhtar
Danny Bailey	Edna Shaw	Makhdoom Chisti
Hannah Hodacs	Muhammad Yusuf	Dorothy Mckenzie
Steve James	Dalal Olewa	Blossom Smith
Ann Molloy	Joe Holyoak	Habib Rehman

A few Officers and local employees also stand out. They include:

Tony Smith	Abdullah Rehman	Pat Wing
Sanjeer Duggal	Anita Halliday	Abdul Hamid

A number of politicians of all parties have paid regular visits to Balsall Heath, have contributed to its success and to the ideas of this book. They include Paddy Ashdown, David Blunkett, Hazel Blears, Oliver Letwin and David Cameron.

I must single out Nowrah for special thanks. She has, without complaint, typed and re-typed the pages which follow time after time as I tweaked and then re-tweaked them. Thanks are owed to her for being so patient and persistent and for making the book readable.

Finally, I must thank my wife, Gill and daughters Sophie and Jane. Too often I was in Balsall Heath or writing this book and not paying enough attention to them. So, they are due both my apologies and my thanks.

I do hope that the words which follow suitably capture all the fine deeds, efforts and suggestions of all the above. All the best bits are due to them. The mistakes are mine.

SPONSOR'S FOREWORD

Dr Dick Atkinson was asked to write this important book by the Chamberlain Forum, Birmingham's own Think Tank. The Forum was set up a few years ago by a number of Birmingham's 'doers' and 'thinkers' to highlight and develop the important work, which is proceeding way beyond the confines of London. Indeed, it is our belief that the work proceeding in the regions is often in advance of that in the Capital and can and should inform it.

Everyone in every political party and in many neighbourhoods wants to know the answer to this question: "How do you renew a struggling neighbourhood?" To date, many have tried and many have failed. Some of these failures have been very costly Government ones. So, we asked Dr Atkinson to tell us the answer based on the work done in Balsall Heath which had been Birmingham's least attractive priority neighbourhood and is now one of its most desirable ones.

"What are the secrets of its success?" we asked. "How can they be replicated?" "Who needs to do what?" "How do you engage a diverse neighbourhood, realise its talents and gain its commitment to change?" We offer you his answers in this book. We believe they should now be built into the policies of both Government and Opposition and adopted by many neighbourhoods.

Steve Botham
Chair, The Chamberlain Forum

INTRODUCTION

Over half of the population of the country live in some 3,000 inner and outer city neighbourhoods where social life leaves much to be desired. Each neighbourhood contains between 5,000 and 20,000 people. But, they experience high crime and the fear of crime, litter and graffiti. Youngsters loiter on street corners and make adults and the elderly anxious.

Difficult families make life in some streets chaotic. There is not much social life and few people have any confidence that things can get better. However, whilst most are resigned to living in poor social circumstances, they would still like to live fuller and happier lives. That's why they are discontent with representative democracy. They feel it should produce better results. But, it doesn't and as a result, few people vote, especially in local Council elections. That is, as well as the streets and public spaces being blighted, so also is democracy. There is a social recession which is just as serious as the economic one.

Why is social life so poor for so many? Why are people so resigned to that social poverty? And, how can things be improved? How can we create social capital and build the Big Society in place of the fractured one we have? This book asks and tries to answer these vital questions.

In doing so it looks closely at Balsall Heath, a once decaying inner ring neighbourhood in Birmingham and charts its successful renewal. It spells out the lessons to be learned from that success and applies them both to other neighbourhoods and to Government.

It also looks at the many costly renewal initiatives by which successive governments have tried to renew neighbourhoods, spells out why they have failed and shows what needs to be done to achieve success.

One reason why Government initiatives have failed is because they were designed to do things 'for' people, not with them. They did not engage or motivate the people who live in the neighbourhoods we describe. And, in turn, residents have expected the State to solve their problems for them. They grumble and don't vote because it doesn't.

This book argues that a key part of the answer to improvement in fact lies in the hands and heads of the people themselves. Given confidence and belief in a better future, they can play a major part in changing their own neighbourhood. Thus, the answer does not rest with Government or more money but in more people using their own unused talents. That is, people have become a major underused asset. So, how can we now realise that asset?

This Third World question is relevant. It asks: "How do you feed a hungry person?" It reminds us that: "If we give them a fish, then it feeds them for a day. But, this makes them dependent on us to give them another one tomorrow. If, however, we teach them how to fish, then it feeds them for life. Plus, it makes them independent and proud – and it frees us to do other things."

The next question to answer follows automatically. It is this: "If people do become active and become their own solution, what are the implications for Government? Does it too have to change and, in so doing, can people come to appreciate it more and vote in greater numbers? Could it be good for democracy? Could it even be that more people vote?"

The chapters that follow pose and try to answer these difficult questions.

1. The problem facing troubled urban areas

This chapter points out that there are now more troubled neighbourhoods than when very well funded renewal initiatives started over 50 years ago. It demonstrates that the failure to solve the problem is due to our having misdiagnosed the nature of that problem. We saw it as being material deprivation when, in fact, it was social deprivation, poverty of the spirit.

2. Re-building the village of Balsall Heath

Explains in some detail the practical steps taken in Balsall Heath in Birmingham's inner ring, which led to its successful transformation. It draws the lessons of that success.

3. Changing people changes places

Shows that the best way of changing and improving places is to change and motivate people.

4. The Community Organiser – building from the bottom-up

Spells out the role of the Community Organiser who is needed to motivate people in the neighbourhoods where they live and to re-create a spirited and caring village life.

5. The crucial role of faith: Can it move mountains?

Explains that if we want to motivate people and develop more spirited neighbourhoods then we must revalue the role of faith in everyday life.

Statistics are provided, which show that in Balsall Heath faith really has moved mountains.

6. Changing the top-down

Explains just how much the structures and budgets of the State must change from 'doing' to 'enabling' in order to respond positively to newly empowered residents. It demonstrates that each neighbourhood needs a Manager to partner the Community Organiser.

7. Neighbourhood Budgeting – and asset management

Looks at what is entailed in disentangling a neighbourhood's budget from the far larger ones with which statutory providers have operated over large tracts of administrative land. For, when these sums are made neighbourhood specific, the resident customer, Community Organiser and Neighbourhood Manager can use them to shape services and make them far more cost effective.

8. Reinventing Government to enable the renewal of neighbourhoods

Asserts that reforming the State and building social capital requires both determined leadership and a new, neighbourhood specific, department of State which is specifically designed to champion Civil Renewal.

9. Renewing Moral Authority

Shows why the State must give a moral lead and help to change the national culture if it is to succeed in also changing its structures to support civil renewal.

10. Politics, culture and renewal

Points out that recovering from the social recession requires a new kind of elected politician at local and national level and a new kind of non-party politics.

11. The way forward – a programme of action

Spells out a little of what a programme of action to drive social renewal might look like.

12. Conclusion

The book concludes that the changes needed to cure the social recession and sustainably renew social life in urban areas are substantial. First, the resident must move from being a passive recipient of services and benefits, a receiver of fish, to being an active shaper of them, a fisherman. Indeed, we will discover that newly active residents in confident neighbourhoods prevent some problems from arising, which in the past, expensive services had been required to tackle.

That is, strong, assertive residents who are good fishermen reduce the need for some services and save money. Thus, freed from supplying so many fish, enlightened Statutory Partners will, in future, 'invest to save' in residents and help to produce 'more for less'. In this context we can see that the well intended Welfare State which Beveridge helped to create to tackle material 'want' and 'squalor' inadvertently also made people socially dependent on that State and less able to help and care for each other. We conclude that in future we need a Welfare Society in which a new and effective State does less 'for' and 'to' people and actively 'enables' them to help themselves and each other in a new partnership of equals. Read on .....

Chapter 1

THE PROBLEM FACING
TROUBLED URBAN AREAS

For over 50 years successive Governments have recognised that a major problem faces very many urban areas. Residents in literally thousands of neighbourhoods have been dissatisfied with and complained about their life circumstances. So, Government after Government have introduced initiative after initiative to make life better, but to little avail. For, in 2001 the new Social Exclusion Unit reported that there were now more excluded, troubled neighbourhoods than before the initiatives started. Why? How can this be?

We have assumed for a long time that the problem faced by urban areas was material poverty. Thus, we have created a solution aimed at solving that problem. But, in practice, the solution has not worked. So, could it be that we have misdiagnosed the problem, and that we need to prescribe a quite different kind of solution?

The symptoms of the urban problem

- Two hundred experts recently combined to say: "Childhood is being eroded by a relentless diet of advertising, addictive computer games, test-driven education and poor child care … Children's well-being and mental health are being undermined by the pressures of modern life". (Telegraph, September 23rd 2011).
- A UN report in 2011 said that 'British parents (are) trapping children in a cycle of compulsive consumerism.'
- Churches across the country are on the brink of bankruptcy and are unable to afford repairs after being repeatedly attacked by thieves stealing metal. "British Transport Police estimate that metal theft now accounts for between 7,000 and 10,000 crimes a month". (Times September 23rd 2011).
- The Sunday Times of September 30th, 2011 told us that in:

> 1901 there were 23,670 priests in the Church of England
> 1961 there were 15,391 priests in the Church of England
> 1985 there were 12,672 priests in the Church of England
> 2010 there were 8,139 priests in the Church of England

- The number of single parent families has been increasing every year for several decades. The number of children in single families has risen from 2.9 million to 3.1 million in the last 10 years (Office for National Statistics). That is, the number of children growing up with only one pair of hands to guide them and without a male role-model has been steadily increasing.
- 'Gang culture', say leading experts, 'provides lost youngsters, especially boys, with a sense of belonging and identity, which they have failed to find at home.'
- In the summer of 2011 we all watched in horror as many thousands of youngsters, largely in gangs, rioted in the streets of London, Liverpool, Birmingham and a worrying number of other cities. They broke into shops, set fire to buildings and houses and caused billions of pounds worth of damage to property and lost goods.
- Many of those who claim benefits do so legitimately. But, large numbers who claim benefits are not entitled to them. They are fit and healthy but play the system of 'hand-outs' for all it's worth. Panorama calculated that they cost the tax-payer up to £20 billion a year. But, it is also the case that many of those who legitimately claim benefits can become used to them and see them as being an alternative to work and earning an income. This 'life on benefits' becomes an alternative to real work and gainful employment and exploits those who are in work who pay for it via their taxes. This is sad, unproductive and contributes to a deep malaise at the core of modern society.
- The quality of life in very many inner and outer city neighbourhoods is unsatisfactory to the majority of people who live in them. Anti-social behaviour is widespread and intimidating. Not only are people afraid to walk the streets at night, but day light shows us that these streets are litter strewn, that graffiti abounds and that gardens and public open spaces are ill-maintained. Few, if any, voluntary agencies exist in many neighbourhoods and communal life is at a very low ebb.
- Some families where the parent(s) is on benefits and an older son is in prison can cost upwards of £70k/year.
- Many people in such areas die up to 10 years sooner than the national average.

Very large sums have been, and are spent by the Welfare State and thus, by the tax payer on providing services for decaying urban neighbourhoods in a sustained attempt to improve the quality of life in them. These services include:

- Public Housing
- Health
- Policing, courts and prison
- Schools and youth provision
- Social Services
- Welfare Benefits

But, despite such spending day in day out by mainstream budgets on mainstream services, the symptoms of the major problem indicated above have prevailed and worsened. The whole village, which tradition tells us is needed to educate the child and steer it to adult maturity and responsibility, has been reduced to the single parent family and the influence of the gang. We are in the grip of a social recession which is just as real and serious as the economic one which we face.

Government Solutions

Successive Governments have known since the 1960's that a major problem exists. To give them credit, each Government in turn has attempted to address the problem with a succession of very well intentioned and well funded initiatives. These have been provided by Central Government on top of existing mainstream funding.

Older readers will remember Urban Aid and Inner City Partnership in the 1960's and 70's. Younger ones will recall the Social Regeneration Budget No 1, then 2, 3, 4, 5, 6, 7 and 8 and New Deal for Communities, each with £50m. Most recently, we witnessed several years of Neighbourhood Renewal Fund and Working Neighbourhoods Fund.

Together, these initiatives have spent many billions of pounds on top of the very large existing mainstream Welfare State budgets described above. But, with some alarm, the Social Exclusion Unit reported early in the new twentieth century that despite all these billions spent over 50 plus years there were now more difficult and excluded neighbourhoods than ever before. That is, despite all the money and all the initiatives, the problem identified above has got worse, not better. The social recession has deepened.

Has the very latest coalition Government initiative, the Big Society, at last made a difference? Unfortunately, the Public Administration Select Committee reported in September of 2011 that 'Volunteering and community participation is at a 10 year low.' The Government's most senior advisors reported that they were "exasperated and appalled" by "Civil Servants who are blocking the implementation of the Big Society agenda." The committee concluded that: "without a comprehensive plan for cross-departmental reform in Whitehall, plans for public services reform, the Big Society, localism and decentralisation will fail". (Telegraph September 22nd 2011).

Oops! Oh dear!

How can it be that the problem has got worse not better despite the enormous existing sums spent each and every year on providing services to people in urban areas, plus the very large sums spent on successive top-down renewal initiatives?

What has caused the problem?

Until now, most Politicians and Governments have seen the problem as being caused by material poverty and inequality and that the re-distribution of wealth from the rich to the poor and the spending of ever more money on topping-up existing services will ease the situation and solve the problem.

Indeed, undoubtedly this has helped to alleviate material poverty. People who once did not have a house, a School to which to send their children, a home for the elderly etc, etc, now do have one. But, wait! Reflect on the old Third World saying which asks: "How do you feed a hungry person?" It says: "Give them a fish and you feed them for today. But, you also make them dependent on you to give them another one tomorrow." It continues:

"If instead, you teach them how to fish, then you feed them for life and make them feel independent and proud. Thus, it frees you from 'doing' things 'to' people and turns you into an 'enabler' and it's cheaper."

Sir William Beveridge is credited with giving the Welfare State a defining boost in the 1930's when he reported that there were 5 great sins which faced society. These included 'ignorance' and 'disease'. Schooling for all into the late teens and the Health Service followed. He also identified 'want' and 'poverty' which laid the foundation for our system of benefits. But, inadvertently we now know that these also multiply the scale of his fifth sin, 'idleness'. For, in providing people with the fish of benefits, it did indeed make people dependent and idle. Again, as the saying informs us, this in turn requires us to provide more and more expensive fish and prevents people from seeing the need to fish for themselves.

So, in doing good things 'to' people, the very well intentioned Welfare State has both helped to alleviate material poverty and, at the same time, created a social dependence, a passivity, a social problem, a social recession. Has this social problem been made more serious by any other factors? Indeed, it has. They include:

- **The pace of Technological Change**

  This has not helped. Of course, washing machines and all sorts of other technologies including I.T, have their beneficial side. But, they also combine to quicken the pace of life so much that past certainties faded and life became governed by the need to grasp and consume the latest fad – even if you have to break a shop's plate glass window to get it as part of a rampaging mob.

- **Demographic Changes**

  The pill and the pace of life have combined to shrink the once common extended family into the modern nuclear family and, beyond that, to the single parent one.

  Many young girls become single parent mothers in their teens, fail to learn parenting skills from their mother and lack the support of either a man or an extended family of aunts, uncles and grandparents. Thus, another old saying is undermined: "It takes a whole village and many pairs of hands to educate a child and lead it into adult maturity." However brave and determined a single mother might be, it is difficult for just two pairs of hands, let alone one, to perform the watching, caring, brief of the whole village. Children suffer. Little wonder that some choose the sense of belonging which a gang provides in place of the one the extended family once provided.

- **The culture of relativity**

  The advent of the Enlightenment also had major benefits. The modern Age of Reason which it introduced supplanted the total dominance in life of subjective and traditional values. It enables science and a whole range of technical and material advances to proceed which prolonged life and made it materially richer. But, there was also a down-side to it.

  Scientific reason and relativity did not just enable man to understand and use the material and objective world more effectively. It also spilled over into the social and subjective world and questioned the ultimate and religious values by which mankind has lived for thousands of years. Those ultimate values had bound people together in mutual care. But, this culture which had been driven and unified by moral values became replaced by one which unleashed a culture of: 'me, mine, I want it now.' It atomised the village. It cut the bonds which held it together.

Any one of the above points carries with it both a materially beneficial dimension and a socially worrying one. However, consider them not in isolation, but intertwined and inter-dependent. Thus, we can see that their combined effect on the moral richness of human life, on the social merits of the extended family and the whole village which the child needs to give them a moral purpose and a sense of belonging and individual worth has been very negative indeed.

Little wonder that the 50 year long succession of costly time-limited Government initiatives issued on top of existing mainstream services has had little effect. They did not counteract these trends. They did not engage the customer. They failed to teach people how to fish. They were gone before they could re-work and re-model struggling mainstream services. As a result, over a 50 year period we have, in effect, wasted many billions of pounds barking up the wrong tree. Just how many billions? It would be salutary and, no doubt, disturbing to know just how large this sum is.

The problem facing urban areas re-defined

It is neither possible nor desirable to rewind our historical clock. Indeed, we must go out of our way not to do so. The Enlightenment was good, technological and medical innovation are good. The Welfare State was a wonderful creation. Quite literally, life has been prolonged and made materially richer because of them. We must make sure we preserve and develop these material virtues.

At the same time, however, we must be careful not to let material advance intrude into or undermine our social life. We must preserve and develop that life and find a way by which material calculation and pure reason can co-exist with and complement subjective logic and the purpose and point which ultimate values give to life.

That is, until now we have failed to see that a key feature of the problem which has reduced our urban life is not material but social poverty. Indeed, we have inadvertently allowed the enriching of our material wealth and the creation of the Welfare State to render us socially and morally poorer, if not actually socially bankrupt.

Is 'socially bankrupt' too strong a phrase? Have we gone too far? Consider those thieves who take the lead from Church roofs and windows and render them unusable. Consider the thousands of youngsters who pelted the Police with stones while breaking into shops and setting fire to houses. Contemplate those families and youngsters who hold entire estates to ransom with their anti-social behaviour. Consider those invisible youngsters whose parents or parent consider only their own needs and leave their children to find their own lonely way forward, and we can see that key features of our society and neighbourhoods within it really have become socially bankrupt. The village which we all need is troubled. It struggles to play its role.

If this is the real problem, then the prescription which might solve it must entail finding ways of building not economic but social capital, of paying homage to and encouraging Social Entrepreneurs in the way that, in the past, we have lauded Economic Entrepreneurs. We must re-build the urban village in modern mode. If we are to end the social recession, then we must build social capital, social riches.

If the great sins of the last century which Beveridge identified in the 1930's included want, poverty and idleness, what are the great sins of this new century? They still include 'idleness'. But, do we now need to add 'isolation' and 'dependency' to it? Are, therefore, the solutions 'engagement', 'belonging' and 'independence'? If so, how do we engender them? In place of a 'doing' Welfare State, which provided people with fish, do we need an equally active Welfare Society, which teaches them how to fish and to be independent and proud?

The chapters which follow are devoted to showing how this has been done in one impoverished neighbourhood, Balsall Heath, and how success there and in a limited number of other neighbourhoods can be replicated in most places. In so doing, we must look carefully at the Welfare State and consider how it can be turned from 'a provider of fish to passive residents' into an 'enabler, a teacher, a liberator'. In a word, can it be helped to find a new role and evolve into a Welfare Society which enables us to complement material wealth with social wealth? In place of 'idleness' can it help to engender engagement, belonging and independence? Can we end the social recession, build social capital and create social riches? And, if so, can we afford it? What will social capital cost in terms of economic capital?

Chapter 2

RE-BUILDING THE VILLAGE
OF BALSALL HEATH

Introduction

This chapter explains how the once tattered and torn inner city neighbourhood of Balsall Heath in Birmingham re-built itself socially. This was not easy and it did take time, thirty years, a generation. But, while Government spent billions on time-limited top-down renewal initiatives in other neighbourhoods, which failed to produce lasting results, Balsall Heath succeeded. So, we must ask: How did it do this? What were the steps it took? And, is it sustainable and replicable elsewhere?

Balsall Heath, a potted history

For those who do not know it, as its name implies, Balsall Heath was once heathland dotted with farms some 130 years ago. Just half a mile from Birmingham's City Centre, its fields were sold and filled with terraced housing to accommodate those who came to staff the industrial and manufacturing revolution.

Once independent of Birmingham, it became included in the City in return for the building of a Baths, Library and Schools. It flourished. Its white working class population was proud and mutually supportive.

Then, after 100 years of development, came the end of Birmingham's metal-bashing manufacturing industries. Those who could do so moved out to more affluent areas. The planners condemned many of the terraced houses, purchased them, rehoused even more residents in other parts of Birmingham, built more municipal houses and created the space for newcomers from Ireland, Africa, the Caribbean and Asia. The factors identified in chapter one added to the difficulties faced by residents.

The once cohesive village became dispersed, atomised and weak. People did not know or understand each other's culture. For decades, just one red light street had been used by a few prostitutes. In the 60's and 70's the village of Balsall Heath became so weak that the dim red light spread until

450 prostitutes patrolled its street corners and thousands and thousands of kerb crawlers made ordinary residents lives miserable. Pimps enticed vulnerable young girls and boys into the trade. Balsall Heath became Birmingham's least desirable neighbourhood. Proud residents who still lived there denied that they did so. But, they couldn't move. For, nobody would buy their house. Houses had become valueless. Residents were stuck. Their problems multiplied:

- The streets became drab and litter strewn.
- Alleyways became overgrown and unusable.
- The 5 small parks in the neighbourhood also became unusable by ordinary folk. They were dominated by drug dealers and gangs.
- Public housing looked drab and uncared for. Gardens looked wild. Hedges became overgrown.
- Residents 'kept themselves to themselves'. They felt powerless and uncared for.

A few intrepid souls went to the Police and the Council in 1980 and pleaded: "Help us. Life is terrible." The answer they got was: "We've been trying. We can't. So, if you don't like it, move. There's nothing we can do." The steps which follow tell us what happened next and its implications for the renewal of neighbourhoods throughout the whole country.

Painfully slowly at first and with few resources, a growing number of residents took the first faltering steps towards rebuilding the social fabric of their area themselves. The small steps have taken 30 years to form a path, which has lead to the sustainable renewal of today.

Had we known then what we know now, these steps might have been taken more deliberately. Had we had greater resources, the steps might have been swifter. But, even with a fair wind, it would only have been possible to shorten the 30 years to say 20, a generation. For, while a Village Hall can be built in a year, the "whole social village, which is needed to fill that hall and educate the child" and see it graduate into adult maturity and care for the elderly does take a generation.

The steps – one by one

1. The creation of a social enterprise

A local trades unionist, Ted, had persuaded the managers of the factory in the centre of Birmingham where he worked to turn a derelict space at the back of it into a recreation area for his fellow workers. On sunny days they took their sandwiches outside to eat and play games of football. In the street where Ted lived was a disused scrap-yard full of litter and rubble. Applying the lesson learned at work to his home, he persuaded some neighbours to scrape the rubble into a heap, bury it with soil and turn it into an adventure playground for youngsters to use who had no-where else to play but the street corner.

Encouraged by that success, Ted approached the vicar of the local St Paul's Church whose congregation had dwindled to 6 to consider opening his disused Church Hall as a pre-school nursery for the children of the young mothers who he knew would like to return to work. Together, they approached a few charities and raised the money to employ trained staff with the help of modest fees, which they asked the mothers to take out of their new wages.

Fast forward 30 years and this fledgling project has developed into St Paul's Community Development Trust, which now also runs an animal farm with sheep, goats, turkeys, rabbits and a host of animals which are the pride and joy of the area. In the spring of 2011 the female sheep bore the first lamb to be born in a hundred years on the Heath. It became a star attraction.

Street Watch

Raja, another Trades Unionist, refused to accept the inevitability of the fact that prostitutes regularly sat on his garden wall as they flagged down kerb-crawlers and touted for business. His family was just growing up and he couldn't let them go out to play or allow their friends to visit. He was ashamed and bitterly resented the authorities who had told him and others: "Sorry, there's nothing we can do. If you don't like it, move."

He talked with friends and neighbours. He pointed out that he was good at organising a picket of management at work to gain better working conditions. So, he reasoned, why not organise a picket of his own street corner, stare at the kerb-crawlers, ostentatiously write down their registration numbers and shame them away.

Before long, there were 20 groups of six or so residents on 20 nearby street corners all following his lead. They took out their kitchen chairs, sat on them, drank tea, ate biscuits and, whenever a kerb-crawler stopped, they'd gently say: "We have your number. Don't come back."

Again, cutting the story short, it took 5 years of concerted Street Watch action reclaiming street after street, evening after evening, weekend after weekend. But, once the 'demand' had gone, the 'supply' soon dwindled until it too disappeared. And, no, it didn't go to another residential area. For, no other area had a red-light image. The problem simply shrank and disappeared.

We all know that major businesses have come together to form BitC (Business in the Community) to help troubled neighbourhoods. But, Balsall Heath witnessed the birth of TUitC (Trades Unions in the Community). Volunteer neighbours enjoying themselves on their own street corners solved a problem that the Police's own Vice-squad, which cost £350k per year couldn't solve. They became known as Street Stewards in imitation of their work place equivalents, Shop Stewards.

Encouraged by the success of St Paul's Trust and Street Watch, more and more residents gradually saw the point of taking action to improve their lives and those of their neighbours.

2. Broken windows, hedges, gates, alleyways, graffiti, dumping

As the saying goes, if a broken window is left unmended, the body language says 'nobody cares'. It invites other windows to be broken. So, a volunteer handy-person or two were identified by residents to:

- Mend broken windows
- Trim overgrown hedges
- Fit gates to gardens and side entryways
- Clear overgrown alleyways
- Remove graffiti
- Clear dumped rubbish
- Organise litter picks

After a while, 2 local people became permanently employed by their fellow residents on these tasks. They became called: "Two men and a van". Their motto is: "We won't do it for you. We will do it with you." More and more people began to care for their environment.

But, above all, Two Men and a Van showed residents that improvements can be made, that 'together we can make a difference', that it's worth staying and investing effort in the neighbourhood.

3. Confused Spaces

Balsall Heath is littered with what residents call 'confused spaces'. There are some 70 of them. Some are as small as 3 by 3 metres. Some are larger, perhaps 20 by 20 metres. Many, but not all of them appeared in Urban Renewal days when the Council was knocking down some of the 100 plus year old housing and putting new ones in their place. The architect and planner of the day thought that it would be attractive to create corner patches of grassed space to brighten the area.

The idea was good. But, before long everyone had forgotten which bit of the Council or other statutory player owned the land and, thus, who should be maintaining it. They became derelict and uncared for. Hence, they became called 'confused' spaces. The weeds grew in them. Litter blew into them and was not cleared. This, in effect, invited people to use them as a dumping ground. This wasn't very nice for the area as a whole. But, it was horrible if you lived adjacent to one.

Residents began to wonder: "If nobody recalls that they own them, why don't we claim "finders keepers?" One by one, next door residents have reclaimed them, maintained them, turned them into flower or shrub beds. It has made a world of difference. In later chapters we will also discuss 'confused finance' and 'confused assets' and the need to take ownership of them.

4. The village is covered by 11 residents groups

First one, then more resident groups were formed until the whole area was covered. Each group covers just 3 or 4 streets, meets every 2 months and agrees what needs to be done. As some 30 people attend each group, this means that 30 X 11 = 330 people regularly meet and either tackle small jobs themselves or give them to Two Men and a Van or to the statutory authorities who are invited to attend their meetings.

5. Good Neighbours

Each residents group has 2 or 3 particularly good and active neighbours for whom nothing is too much trouble. They visit the elderly, phone the Police to move a dumped car and befriend the lonely. They 'give' a lot and 'receive' much gratitude and respect in return. These Good Neighbours are also called 'Street Stewards'.

6. Communal Meals

Every 2 or 3 months some 300 of the above sit down and eat a meal together. A little community business might be done. But, the main object of the exercise is simply to be together and to eat as one extended family. In a word, the meals help all the players to 'belong' to and 'identify' with each other.

7. Communal Honours

Everyone likes to be patted on the back and thanked. So, a couple of times each year, 6 or so Good Neighbours who have acted above and beyond the call of duty are singled out and thanked at a Communal Meal. Not only does this spur them on to do more. It helps them to be seen as good role models for others. A few years ago there were 5 known Good Neighbours or Street Stewards. Now there are 70.

8. Communal Celebrations

Fireworks nights. Every November 1,500 people gather to watch and enjoy a display of fireworks. "It's good", said one young girl, "It's like we are all just one big family. It puts me on cloud nine for a week."

Carnival. Thirty years ago, 200 people attended the first Carnival held on the village green, one of the small local parks. It was policed by 15 officers on the alert for problems. Last summer 5,000 people attended and 3 police officers staffed a stall, distributing smoke alarms and recruited youngsters into the force.

9. The Calendar and Welcome Packs

Every New Year a Balsall Heath Calendar which is full of local photos and meeting dates is published and pushed through every letter box, all 4,500 of them.

Good Neighbours have a bundle of Welcome Packs which are full of useful information to give to newcomers in the way they once gave a cup of sugar or a jug of milk.

10. The Community Newspaper

Every month a local Community Newspaper (The Heathan for Balsall Heath) is produced and pushed though every letter box. It contains local good news stories and useful information. Its letters page is jammed with requests for action and thanks for deeds well done.

11. Food Hampers

At times of Eid and Christmas, some 300 Food Hampers are distributed to lone elderly folk. The food is collected by the local school children. The hampers are distributed by Good Neighbours and Councillors.

Every week or so the Forum's Neighbourhood Wardens call on most elderly folk for a chat and cup of tea. They also offer to do a bit of shopping or collect a prescription.

12. Volunteers and Active Citizens

Volunteers from local faith groups regularly help the Two Men and a Van to tackle local eyesores. Students from the local secondary school turn the theory of Citizenship in the classroom into good practice in the community by also tackling and improving local parks, car parks and 'confused' spaces.

13. Ward Committee meetings

A few years ago, the 3 local Councillors would meet as a Ward Committee with, perhaps, 3 or 4 residents attending. Today, many residents attend, agree issues to be tackled either by themselves or the Council or other partners. Once these meetings were boring to residents and regarded as being irrelevant. Today, they are exciting, people look forward to them – and the local vote in local elections is rising.

14. The Local Police Station as a 'Solution Centre'

The local Police station happens to be in the very centre of the village. But, its doors were closed to the public. So, residents have voluntarily staffed its front desk and kept it open for several years.

But, it is now also being used as a 'Solutions Centre'. For one day a week, not just the Police but all statutory partners allocate one Officer to be there together. Two things happen as a result:

1. They form a local joint task force and agree common actions.
2. Residents visit and use it as a one-stop-solutions-shop. They bring a problem and leave with a solution.

15. Balsall Heath in Bloom

Naseem travelled first to Solihull, an affluent Birmingham suburb, then to Stratford upon Avon. She was impressed by their planters, hanging baskets, floral displays and the atmosphere of beauty and pride, which they engendered.

She returned to Balsall Heath and asked: "Why can't our streets look like that? Why can't we enter Balsall Heath into the national Britain in Bloom competition? Why can't my children grow up surrounded by this kind of beauty?"

Residents took over a confused space, a derelict patch of Council land of about 40 meters by 70 meters, which resembled a wilderness. They levelled it, dug it over, scrounged two large polythene tunnels and turned the land into a mini garden centre. Over a period of 4 years they built 80 large wooden planters, scattered them around Balsall Heath on street corners and made 250 hanging baskets for houses and corner shops. The area is now a riot of colour all the year round.

More! Ten years ago just 4 residents entered their garden in the neighbourhood's new Annual Gardening Competition. Last year 80 gardens were entered as more and more residents buy seedlings from their own Garden Centre and compete to make their garden special with flowers, fruit and vegetables.

There's still more! Each of the 5 local primary schools now also have their own gardens in their school grounds. Youngsters grow flowers and vegetables, then display them to the Britain in Bloom judges and use some of them to cook a meal for them.

Naseem is pleased. But, so too are all those others who live in Balsall Heath. Visitors come and admire the effect. Some even refuse to believe that they are in one of Birmingham's inner ring neighbourhoods. When Chief Superintendent Phil Kay came to Balsall Heath's Police Station he said: "It's like being in a leafy suburb. This could be Solihull." And it all feels so much safer and cared for. Residents who once denied that they lived in Balsall Heath now proudly proclaim that they do.

16. A Capacity Builder – Community Organiser

None of these steps could have been sustained without a full-time Capacity Builder, a Community Organiser. So, before long residents raised the money to permanently employ their own organiser. Just as the workers in a factory need a Shop Steward to help them to improve their working conditions, so also residents need a 'Street or Community Steward' to help them to improve their living conditions.

17. A neighbourhood Forum or Village Voice

The Community Organiser and Two Men and a Van needed a management committee of residents to employ them and make all of the above activities accountable to the whole neighbourhood. So, the Good Neighbours and resident groups combine to hold area-wide elections. Every year 18 people are chosen to both act as an employer and to represent the area as a whole. If you like, they are the modern equivalent of the elders or wise men of the village of old. Another comparison might be this: A church has a vicar (the Community Organiser) and a Church Council (the Village's Neighbourhood Forum or Council) to ensure that the Church functions well. At first, the residents Forum had just 3 main functions:

1. It represented the area.
2. It built capacity and employed the main Street Steward or Community Organiser.
3. It provided some services like Two Men and a Van and those activities described above.

But, as we shall see in later chapters, before long it developed and began to pose the need for extra activities.

It must be emphasised again that it takes time to make a social difference, to re-build a tattered village. These steps were taken with very little money. For, they were taken by people caring for and supporting each other, as the next chapter emphasises. The next 2 chapters look in turn at the transforming power of active people and at why a Community Organiser is needed to keep them on their toes and well resourced.

Chapter 3

CHANGING PEOPLE CHANGES PLACES

Can you spot the difference? – How do you get...

...from this...

...to this...

...and from this...

...to this?

It's people like these who change places.

And from this, to this...

Before

During

After

The first faltering steps taken in the transformation of Balsall Heath entailed a Trades Unionist, then a Community Organiser nudging first this, then another resident into reaching beyond themselves. Instead of grumbling, shrugging their shoulders and saying 'it's not possible' they were persuaded to have a go and, in so doing, surprised and surpassed themselves.

At first a person might undertake a small task. But, one thing leads to another and bigger and bigger challenges can be accepted. In the process, as the stories in this chapter show, not only are other people and places helped, but the person grows, gains self esteem and the confidence to tackle issues they once imagined to be beyond them.

Mark's story

During my time working at Balsall Heath Forum I have learnt a valuable lesson in life and that there is a much better way to live it. I have come from a life of wrong doing to helping people better theirs. And without the Forum's guidance, I would have not been able to gain this new found way of thinking.

With help from the Forum I have also learnt that by helping others, I can help myself.

I started with the Forum on a Community Punishment Placement. I now have a job there. I'm proud now.

Sajim's story

As I was kicked out of school for 2 days because of bad behaviour, my uncle wanted me to spend some time with the Balsall Heath Forum by helping them send leaflets and cleaning up the area.

At first, I thought this was a punishment for my crime but, as the days went by, I have realised where I had gone wrong and how I could pull my act together before I throw my life away. The Balsall Heath Forum have taught me to be noble; never think that you are better than another person, honest; never lie for any reason and also to put myself in other people's situation and understand where they are coming from.

Overall, the experience I had has been wonderful. I made a couple of new friends who are associated with the Balsall Heath Forum and people on the roads who I have helped. I have learnt a motto which is 'Nobody wants to know a dosser but would be proud to know an educated person'. After the experience I have been through, I am going to focus on my education instead of my friends, at the end of the day my friends aren't going to be there to give me money or to look after me so I have to make something of myself.

By Sajim Ahmed

Queensbridge School

PC Kidner's story

I would like to start by personally thanking Hamid, Abdullah, Sajid, Sulayman and all of the other Forum staff who so kindly received me and devoted their time to showing me what the Forum was about and what role they perform for the community.

Before attending I do not mind admitting that I had some misconceptions regarding the area, which stemmed from the opinions of others and ignorance more than anything else.

Balsall Heath has had historical issues, notably prostitution, drug misuse and I think this formed part of my view about the area.

Today has been a real eye-opener for me, how wrong I was! The fantastic dedication and effort by the Forum staff was obvious by the friendly and warm way we were received by members of the public whilst out on patrol. No matter what ethnic background, everyone we encountered was very positive about the work they do including sorting out problems themselves if they can, or referring the problem to the correct public service contact if they could not.

I actually wish I was as warmly received and greeted where I live as I was in Balsall Heath!

Thank you all for a truly valuable experience and I am very much looking forward to policing the area and regard the Balsall Heath Forum as an imperative resource to assist me in doing so. They are a vital link between us (the Police), the other public service organisations (Fire/Ambulance service, various Council Departments) and the community.

PC 20660 Kidner

Sophie's story

I come from the other side of Birmingham. I'd just like to say thank you to the Forum's Warden for his excellent personal support and the £20 he gave me from his own pocket just when I needed it most. I'd crashed my car and was desperate without a penny. Not many people would help a stranger on her own and give kindness like that without a thought. He didn't know whether I'd come back and return it. He just gave without thought of return. That's special.

Keep up the good work and honesty.

Thank you so much.

PC Field's story

Community Placement at Balsall Heath Forum

The work being done by the Wardens (and others) at the Forum has astounded me. They work tirelessly to forge links between the many agencies and the local community. Schemes such as 'the walking bus' are clearly invaluable and are installing high standards in children at a very young age.

The Wardens assist local residents with a vast range of issues and are even known to perform gardening tasks and rubbish collections in a bid to make streets cleaner and safer for all who use them.

The local community seem to like and respect the Wardens which is evident when they patrol with the many people who greet them along the way and address any issues they may have.

The local Police must be benefiting from the work of the Wardens in the manner in which the Wardens can reach residents who may still consider the Police to be unapproachable.

The work being done by the people at the Forum has really impressed me and opened my eyes to local issues. There are very visible results being achieved by the Wardens and Balsall Heath is evidentially a much better community for their presence.

PC Hobday's story

I am currently a student Officer for the West Midlands Police Force and today I have come on my community attachment with the Balsall Heath Forum. I must comment that my experience today has been a great eye opener, the relationship the staff have with the local communities are fantastic and they also have some exceptional ideas to involve communities and to bring people from all walks of life together. The staff are fantastic and have made me feel very welcome and my personal opinion is that other groups and communities could learn a lot from groups like the Balsall Heath Forum.

Thank you for the opportunity.

Naseem's story

I hear lots of people talking about capacity building and social capital and I know it means different things to different people.

I started in a job in the nursery next door to the Balsall Heath Forum and I was asked to come and attend a new meeting they were setting up for local Asian women as Asian women were not getting involved in any of the residents groups the BH Forum was setting up. When I went to the first meeting I was told the BHF was a 'capacity building organisation'. Hmmm.... I thought.

Well after attending a few meetings and making new friends at the meetings we all agreed that as women we had nowhere we could call our own, a place to meet and do things! Through the discussions we decided we wanted a women's centre for local women. The Forum offered me a chance to develop this idea into a reality.

We decided on a name for the women's Group – Saheli – it means friends in Urdu/Punjabi/Gujarati. We contacted 236 local women and through a feasibility study, we established that local women wanted to have a 'women's only centre, run by women for women'. They wanted to do fitness, exercise and swimming! Cutting an eight year story short Balsall Heath now has its very own (and very successful) Women's Centre called the Saheli Adventure Hub. Women from all ages and backgrounds, religions and cultures all take part in exercise, walking, biking, canoeing and so much more. There are many women who have not just become physically active but are active in the community taking part in consultations, local ward meetings and even becoming Governors of local schools.

I was employed at the BH Forum for eight years. It's the longest job I have ever had. Through that time I have learned about partnership working, relationship building with service providers, communities, organised community groups, running and taking part in effective meetings and supporting many other women to take up short courses to get involved. Through all this 'learning and building' I have completed an HNC in Business and an MSc in Regeneration Policy and Research. For the BH Forum has achieved a lasting change for residents. It shows that if residents are active partners then the democratic processes/solutions lead to long term sustainable change for all the residents of Balsall Heath. That's what 'capacity building and social capital' now means to me. If I can't do or change something, I know others in my community that can.

Raja's story

I worked as a shop steward on the railways and lived and raised my family in Balsall Heath and wondered about moving because it was so awful. Then I went to a Forum meeting and thought: What if I applied Trade Union practices not just at work but to where I lived. I could organise my friends and neighbours and help them to reclaim the streets and parks and make them safe.

I've been doing that now for 18 years and the place is so much better it's not true. Plus, I'm now a Magistrate, MBE and was the elected chair of the Forum for several years. It helps to represent the whole area. I'm really pleased and proud of what I've done and become and so are my family.

I'd like to think that my own story tells other people in Balsall Heath that they too can and should: Think big, the sky is the limit. If we do things together there's nothing we can't achieve and aspire to. There is an old Trade Union saying: 'There's strength in Unity'. But, in Balsall Heath we don't just apply it to the place where we work. We also apply it to the place where we live. More should do this. Then, we'd make lots of neighbourhoods better.

Sanjeer's story

Four years ago I was up to no good, on drugs and in trouble with the police. I hung around with the wrong crowd.

I had a choice – do time or come to the Forum. I chose the Forum. Since then I've made friends and met new people who have been a much better influence on me.

What I'm doing now is right and it makes me feel good and at peace with myself. Lots of people tell me to keep up the good work of tidying the area, growing and planting our plants. They cheer me on and it feels great and I know it influences for the good others who could go the wrong way.

Where would I be now if I hadn't gone with the Forum and my new friends? I dread to think.

Bernard's story

I'm 75 and I've got 2 dogs and I live in a Council flat. I couldn't open my back door to the garden because a tree grew against it. So, my dogs used my flat as a loo. It smelt horrible. Social Services wanted to put me in a home and put the dogs to sleep.

The Forum found out and cleared my garden, cleaned and painted my flat and I can manage now. The volunteers who did my garden were a God send. I'd have died in a home and lost my 2 dogs.

But, my real life saver goes to the Forum office staff, Rozie and Carrie. I get them to do my forms and letters. I can't see well. But they mother me and I call them my aunties. Nothing is ever too much trouble, like cleaning all the dogs mess from my kitchen and living room and getting new furniture. Without them, I'd be dead. They are my family. I can't say how much I need them and love them.

Dalal's story

I was unsure of my future and had no direction before I got involved in Saheli Women's Group. Since then I have grown and developed into somebody who is able to speak out about what I think and believe in! I am at the University of Birmingham studying youth and community work and feel that I will go on to do a specialised post graduate qualification. Before, I never had the support and push I needed to enable me to do further education and I am the first female in my family to have done so. I have had inspiring examples around me of how education is important to get further in life and do the work that I am passionate about.

I now hope myself to inspire and help motivate other young people within my own Yemeni community just like I have been enlightened to further myself. There are many barriers but I think it is our responsibility to help young people grow and ask questions about what they are taught and take control of things that affect them.

I started off a shy and intimidated young girl and have progressed to a confident and informed young woman due in part to Saheli Women's group that exits in my local community. I think I will work within the field to help make the changes necessary to eradicate the barriers that exists within the current systems.

Abdullah's story

My transition from being a self employed businessman to Community Warden has been challenging and rewarding.

It all began when my partner and brother decided to relocate the family corner-shop. I did not want to be stuck behind a counter for another 15 years. So, we decided to part ways and I ended up taking a job at the Forum.

All my life I had given instructions to others and been a Manager. So, it was a shock to my system when I had to take orders. My attitude was about to change forever.

Ordinary people in the community looked to my colleagues for guidance and advice on where to get help from. Lots of the time we would simply roll up our sleeves and begin to solve whatever seemingly impossible problem they had.

The more I did this kind of work and watched my partners getting on their hands and knees to help someone, I felt ashamed of myself for feeling I was above doing work like this. I could not initially face those people who had once looked up to me for being self employed, who now saw me wearing my working clothes or my high visibility jacket. I worried about what they would think.

I struggled for some time with my own insecurities, and tried to shield my face as much as possible during any dirty environmental work given to us.

However more and more people began to approach me for help and I was now in a position where I had the facilities to answer their need and the contacts to intervene if I could not help myself. Suddenly the community were accepting me in my new role. It did not look down on me. It looked up to me in a new way.

If I sit back today and think of the first year I spent here, the problems I faced were all mine. If we are humble enough and realise that we are not too good to pick the litter off the street, and shovel up the rubbish from alleyways, we could all be living in a better and stronger community.

If we can put aside our wealth and power, and knock on our neighbour's door to ask how they are, then we can recreate the best values, which make us interdependent.

I have lost my arrogance and graces by meeting and being in daily contact with some amazing individuals, and one day we can get a community where each of us look out for others regardless of wealth and status.

It
takes
a
Whole Village
to
Educate a Child
=
Changing people changes places

These personal stories tell one common tale for those interested in neighbourhood renewal. It is this:

For the whole of the last century we have tried to do good things for poor people by providing them with services and physical assets. But, we have delivered these in top-down, one-size-fits-all, ways over large tracts of land and not the small places, the neighbourhoods or villages, in which people live and with which they identify.

The serious unintended consequence of this has been that this has turned the resident customer of these services and assets into a passive recipient with no purchase over them. At the same time, the provider has become so remote from the places where people live that the services and assets they deliver are ill maintained and appear uncared for. Thus, more and more neighbourhoods have become bleak and frightening places.

Hitherto, we have wrongly supposed that more money will solve the problem. Thus, renewal initiative after initiative have spent billions – but to little avail because we have not realised that the essential ingredient in caring for people and places are people themselves. The vital message of the photographs and life-stories of this chapter is that we need to enable the passive recipient to become the active participant with a sense of social responsibility and the ability to refashion the services and assets to suit the diverse needs of different neighbourhoods.

Achieving this end does not require more money. It does entail using existing money differently – and changing the way we live and care for each other. It entails empowering people in the neighbourhoods where they live to shape and direct the quality of their lives and public assets.

The best policies in the world and all the money in it will be of no avail if the village where the child is growing up is desolate, its public spaces are not looked after and there is not a sense of mutual friendship or social responsibility. *We need good people not just good policies*. We need a moral compass to guide people on their way to a better life and to give them the courage and vision to make a difference.

A past Chief Constable of the West Midlands, Sir Paul Scott-Lee, was a young policeman in Balsall Heath 20 years ago. Then, it was atomised, desolate and the frightening red light district of Birmingham. He was astonished when he returned eight years ago as the Chief Constable to find it had been transformed. He searched for an explanation of what had made the difference and settled on just 3 words. He said the neighbourhood is now:

- Together
- Confident
- Aspirational

These are the vital values upon which a vibrant urban village can be constructed. More, if these values can be conjured to reality in Balsall Heath, they can be recreated in any troubled neighbourhood in the land by their own Active Citizens. It is time that we gave ourselves the task of finding and resourcing such people if we want to make sure that the next generation has the robust village it needs to support it.

In the past we have spent countless millions of extra pounds on renewal initiatives on top of costly one-size-fits-all services delivered to passive recipients. So, the pounds fell on stony ground and the initiatives were not sustainable.

The vital tale the above stories and photographs tell is that lasting renewal will only happen through changed people, their spirit and enterprise. That is, to cure the social recession we need to build social capital. Material capital alone is insufficient and may even hinder the building of its social equivalent.

Should we Commission Services or invest in a new way of life?

The need to create Social Capital has major implications for the way we think about renewal and encourage it. Much of renewal has, in the past, turned around the need to 'commission services' from the most appropriate supplier. There is some merit in this. For, the Third Sector is often better placed than the public one to deliver services with passion and commitment.

But, this chapter has been all about changing people and creating a caring village in which they can find an identity and purpose. It is about enabling people to live fuller, socially richer lives. This prevents the need for some services. For, in a caring village, there are fewer crimes, less litter, less need to put the elderly into institutions. This not only avoids the need to commission some services, it also saves money.

That is, developing a whole village is not a service. It's a way of life. It can't be commissioned from between competing service deliverers. It has to be grown in the way a family grows. And, it involves everyone. This fact tells us that we have been operating with misleading indicators of success.

Indicators of success

When we focus on services, we come up with one set of indicators. We ask:

*   Are more people in work?
*   Is the arrest rate high?
*   Have we picked up a large amount of litter?
*   Have we mended more broken windows than last year?
*   How many students pass how many GCSE's?

But, when we see the problem as being one of social recession and the solution as being one of re-building social capital we ask:

- Does the neighbourhood look and feel good?
- Are people confident and proud?
- Do people trust one another?
- Are fewer services needed and is money saved? That is, are there now no windows to mend because none are broken?

It seems that as well as looking at the wrong problem and, thus, the wrong solution, we have been looking at the wrong set of indicators of success. We need to concentrate on and measure new ones. So, we end this chapter by refocussing our attention and concentrating less on services and commissioning and more on changing people and creating a whole village and a new way of collective life.

It is very important to acknowledge that this does not just happen by chance or even by policy. Left to their own devices, few people will feel able to do what those described above have done. To reach beyond themselves, to discover hidden virtues, most people need to be nudged by a Ted, Raja or Naseem. The next chapter looks at the role of the Community Organiser.

Chapter 4

THE COMMUNITY ORGANISER – BUILDING FROM THE BOTTOM-UP

Some suppose that it is possible to invite a troubled neighbourhood to renew itself and it will just happen, that the people described above will simply 'get up and go' without further ado or support. Far from it. Life in urban neighbourhoods has been unravelling for decades, people have become passive and unused to shaping events and taking collective action.

Just as an un-unionised factory needs a Ted or a Raja to act as a shop steward and help their fellow workers to become organised and united, so also an Urban Village where people live needs a Street Steward. Some call this person a Capacity Builder or Community Organiser. Call them what you will, each neighbourhood setting out on the path towards recovery needs one. Without one, they will struggle. So, what does the Community Organiser do and how do they do it?

First of all, it is important to note that every neighbourhood has a potential one, if not two or three such people. Merely, in the past, they have simply not been identified, resourced and supported. So, anyone interested in helping a neighbourhood to start the long journey to recovery is advised to resist waiting for some expensive top-down government initiative and to look for the neighbourhood's Ted, Raja or Naseem. They are there, as it were, waiting to be discovered and to discover for themselves just how much they have to offer.

The Job Description of the Community Organiser includes:

Supporting good neighbours – accentuating the positive

It is important to start from small beginnings and slowly lay the foundation upon which bigger things can be built. So, the Community Organiser will wish to start by, for example, helping neighbours who live on either side of a weed infested alleyway to clear it. Or, to find another neighbour who will regularly knock on the door of a lone elderly person to see whether they need some shopping done for them. Or, to link a school which is adjacent to a park with that park and adopt a corner of it as a rose or vegetable garden.

Different neighbourhoods will have different local needs upon which to focus. But, once these needs have been identified and a few Active Residents or Good Neighbours have received support and the satisfaction gained from their act of kindness, it is possible to begin to identify bigger and more challenging neighbourhood-wide issues. Just how many elderly people are there? Should a local agency be asked to take on the neighbourhood-wide role of visiting each and every one of them and providing them with a day-centre? Should Street Watch walk-abouts be organised in areas where residents feel unsafe? Does the negative image of the neighbourhood need to be changed with the help of a positive marketing campaign?

Again, the relevant issues will differ from neighbourhood to neighbourhood. But, in the case of most neighbourhoods, the time will be reached when the Community Organiser can say: "Don't we now need a Neighbourhood-wide Forum or Village Council? For, if we had one it would make what we are doing accountable and representative." More, it would enable us to go to statutory agencies and ask them to listen to and respond to our needs and they'd have to take us seriously.

Just as our Government in Whitehall has evolved, so also each Neighbourhood Forum will evolve from small beginnings to larger and more ambitious ones. So, a major long term goal of the Community Organiser is to help residents to develop to the point where they elect a small number of the most active people to act as representatives of the neighbourhood, in effect to act as mini-councillors.

Dealing with the difficult people – eliminating the negative

A strong community with a number of well organised Active Residents and a Forum can achieve many good things. However, as well as there being good people in every neighbourhood you will also always find a few people who will resist change and oppose the interests of the many. They can be fitted into 4 negative categories.

- Criminals.
- Local figures who were used to ruling the roost when nobody else was involved but who can't cope when lots of people are taking part.
- The professional, such as the teacher who wishes to keep parents out of school because "amateurs have nothing to do with education".

- The Councillor who feels threatened if he or she can't see how bottom-up and top-down can act in partnership.

Experienced Community Organisers will spend much time and effort on trying to include everyone. But, despite every patient attempt to involve everyone, one or two people in one or other of these four categories will resist becoming included. They will go to considerable lengths to maintain their role in the failing status quo and prevent the inclusion and empowerment of the many.

In order to help the large majority to step to the fore, develop their own voice and build a new array of little associations, it is necessary to hold people in these categories at arms length. That is, one of the most fundamental features of Capacity Building is the creation of **space** for people who are shy, lack skills and the confidence to acquire the ability to shape the quality of their lives and contribute to the well being of the community.

Another important feature is **time**. The fabric of industrial and post-industrial neighbourhoods has been unravelling for 50 years. It really will take a generation as well as space to re-knit tattered areas and include excluded people. So, a Community Organiser's job is, in effect, for life.

Tackling the Criminal is not easy. First they have to be identified. They have been so used to ruling the roost and holding unconfident residents in fear that people are reluctant to point them out or 'grass' on them. So, some people must band together and find the collective confidence to pick them out and either shame them into inactivity or persuade the 'powers that be' to arrest them or place an ASBO (Anti Social Behaviour Order) on them.

Those in authority do not live in troubled neighbourhoods. They can feel that acting against the criminal infringes their civil liberties. One definition of a liberal which holds sway in excluded neighbourhoods is: "A person who hasn't yet been mugged".

An abiding image of the James Bulger tragedy was the number of adults who he or his two young abductors passed and who half held out their hands to halt them, yet who drew back in fear of being thought to meddle. Good neighbours, Capacity Builders and Guides must change the relativistic liberal culture which allows 'anything to go' into one which asserts and upholds acceptable standards in public places.

Tackling the sole prominent local figure can also be difficult. In most neighbourhoods there are one or two people who, in the absence of many active people, have pushed themselves to the fore and gained the attention of professionals and councillors.

Some of these, it has to be said, have done a lonely and good job through difficult times. Others have had their egos fed as apparently important people recognised them and paid them attention. They have often been treated as the 'token' resident with whom to 'consult', thus enabling the professional to claim that 'residents' are involved.

This is a sham and a shame. As in old colonial days, many professionals inadvertently keep a very few prominent local people in positions of power and make it very difficult for others to become involved. For, if many people are to participate then the role of the local worthy necessarily shrinks and they become less significant.

The 'token' resident will not be sidelined easily. They will kick up a fuss and make all kinds of claims about those who take their place in order to try to retain their position. It is easy to feel sorry for them and, thus, delay the time when many more people participate. It is far harder to be cruel to be kind and insist that the token resident either adopts a new role which enables others to come forward or step back. Either way, if progress is to be made, the deed must be done. As they say, you can't make an omelette without breaking eggs.

The professional planner and politician. The official can be just as significant an opponent of change as the criminal and token resident. Indeed, because of their status, they can be a greater obstacle.

The 'expert' planner will of course claim that they know best and that the inexpert resident doesn't and shouldn't rock the boat. The 'elected' Councillor or MP may similarly claim that they are the 'accountable person' who must decide while residents, even large numbers of them, are not accountable, thus rendering their views insignificant.

The culture is changing. It is now possible to show the 'expert' that residents know their neighbourhood far better than they do. Like the token resident, it may be similarly possible to show the politician that although they represent a Ward or Constituency they do not represent a social neighbourhood and that those engaged in participatory democracy have a greater legitimacy. If so, fine. But, if not, both planner and politician may have to go. As in business, so in public enterprise, if the planner is not up to the job in hand they may have to be redeployed or downsized and made redundant.

In the case of the politician, they may have to be voted out of office. The election of 2001 saw an independent turn the safe majority of the sitting politician in Kidderminster into a majority for the independent of 18,000. This outcome is likely to be repeated frequently in each year's election for Council places. Active Citizens are beginning to stand in Council elections – about time too.

Renewing neighbourhoods and building social capital does not entail providing more of what exists. On the contrary, it entails changing the way we do things. What exists has been founded on the State and Local Government providing poor, monopolistic, one-size-fits-all services to customers in neighbourhoods who have no choice.

In future, residents must act responsibly and provide more for themselves while the State must (a) 'do' less and (b) 'enable' more. The change from 'A' to 'B' can be pictured as follows:

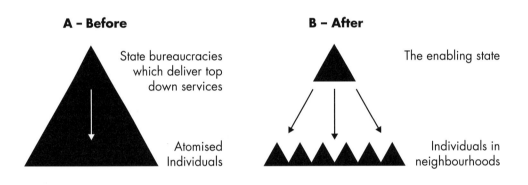

A – Before

State bureaucracies which deliver top down services

Atomised Individuals

B – After

The enabling state

Individuals in neighbourhoods

A glance at the above picture shows just why the professional who was comfortable and used to life within 'A' can feel unsure about what to do within 'B' and may resist the change. There is a gap in the middle of the large pyramid which they once filled.

Building social capital

If eliminating the negative requires **space**, then holding people at arms length who are obstacles to change requires **time**, the time it takes to build up new local associations.

To achieve **space and time**, the Community Organiser requires a **strong** and delicate hand. If the four obstacles described above are to be held at bay whilst unconfident residents are to find the **space** and gain the **time** to build themselves up, then a **firm** and gentle lead is required. **Toughness** is needed to keep the unwanted away and **tenderness** is required to give people the long, slow chance to discover their identity and impose it upon the public arena.

However, space, time, tenderness and toughness are not enough. Local people also need their Community Organiser to find **resources** for them if they are to realise their hopes. These include:

- **An office** and meeting space. At first an empty shop front, old church hall or flat borrowed from a housing association may suffice. Before long, however, any self-respecting community will need something resembling a village hall or Community Centre in which an array of functions can be held.
- **Staff** are also needed. Just one Community Organiser will not satisfy the local appetite for doing things for long. Each neighbourhood will detail its own needs. They might include removing graffiti, removing abandoned cars, hiring a street caretaker, carer for the elderly, staff for a playgroup, a fund-raiser, a person to negotiate with statutory service providers or all of these.
- **Assets** – property – can play a vital part. A mini-bus and truck might be needed by Two Men and a Van, an old school building might be essential for the play-group or elder's club. The users of the park might wish to own it or re-open a disused church as the focal point of life in the neighbourhood. That is, people are not the only underutilised asset in a neighbourhood. A good Community Organiser will identify a variety of disused assets and put them to local use.
- All of these resources will need the **running costs** which cover heat, light and administrative costs as well as the salaries of the staff. A jumble sale or car boot sale might come first. After that a grant will be needed or an investment from an enlightened statutory provider.

With Capacity Building resources such as these, residents who were dependent can come together to form not just 'home-grown' and 'tailor-made' tenants and friendship groups, but nurseries, family centres, job creation schemes, Community Development Trusts and Social Enterprises which deliver services and welfare on a significant scale. These local self-help associations exist in every part of the country, they support the unconfident individual and provide them with a springboard to life.

There are plenty of cases where one person with one idea tried to realise it and struggled but persisted. From such small beginnings major voluntary projects have grown. Maybe 10 or 15 years later, that solitary individual has been joined by hundreds more who combine to run a voluntary sector which spends (and raises) £5m a year. You don't believe it? Visit Royds in Bradford, Coin Street in London, or Castle Vale, Perry Common and Balsall Heath in Birmingham. If they can do it, so can you.

Money

'Ah', you might say, 'but doesn't the Community Organiser cost a bit. How will that cost be covered?'

A later chapter will answer this question in greater detail. Here, it is sufficient to recall that a good Organiser and a strong neighbourhood prevents a variety of problems from arising which would have been expensive to solve. Just one burglary costs £15,000. One elderly person put into an institution costs £60,000 plus.

But, one Organiser costs around £25,000 plus, say, the costs of running a community office and paper work, another £15,000. Total? £40,000. That's 3 burglaries prevented and one elderly person kept in their own home. So, the answer is: There is no need for any external funding. Simply, one or two Statutory Partners who benefit as a result of the Community Organiser's work should see the point of 'investing in them to save'.

Social Sector Trusts and Enterprises

In Liverpool an entire housing estate, the Eldonian Village, complete with a community advice and resource centre, has been built and is run by local people. In Belfast, the Flax Trust has established a health centre, shopping complex, housing association and theatre-job creation scheme. It has a multi-million pound turnover. In Easterhouse, Glasgow, Bob Holman and colleagues have constructed a wide range of self-help associations. The Wise group in Glasgow have generated many dozens of jobs through helping unemployed people to take on services once supplied by statutory service providers. In Bromley by Bow a church now contains a nursery, play group, craft centre and restaurant. By its side is a park, health and advice centre. Bromley by Bow has become an urban village. In addition to Balsall Heath in Birmingham at least one such village now exists in every town or city of the land.

Scattered throughout the country there are now well over 200 Community Development Trusts or Community Enterprises of the kind outlined above. Some became involved in regeneration principally through education. Others became engaged via job creation, housing or the environment. Most are supported by the national Development Trust

Association which has a sister association in Scotland. All end up creating joined-up solutions to a variety of problems regardless of their starting point.

The statistics of the third sector show that it packs a real punch. It accounts for 10% of GDP according to Sir Dennis Landau of the Unity Trust Bank. In Birmingham, Ian Morrison, then Director of its voluntary Council, showed that 49% of voluntary sector funding is self-generating. The third sector can no longer be depicted as Lady Bountiful confined to the back stage of society. It now struts the centre of the stage and has quietly taken on the provision of excellent welfare services which the State could only struggle to deliver. It is capable of undertaking very much more. It holds the key to the recovery of even the most difficult urban areas. Hitherto, the bottom-up progress and achievements described have been made against the 'flow' of the Welfare State. They have been made despite, not because of, the way the top-down has been organised.

Forming a Neighbourhood Forum

If it doesn't already have one, each recovering neighbourhood will soon need its Community Organiser to help to create a Neighbourhood Forum. Without some kind of resident's agency a neighbourhood won't make much progress or be trusted to employ staff, handle money and enter into partnerships with experienced Statutory players. Thus, figuring out how to build a Forum is a very important part of the local Community Organiser's job.

In order to gain widespread local support, a Forum will need to be made up of people who come from the 4 corners of the neighbourhood – it's no good having the Eastside represented but not the Westside. Similarly, it will need women and men, people of different faiths and so on in-order that no group feels excluded.

Getting all these people together isn't easy. It involves a lot of talking, which is a great deal more effective than leafleting. The process is helped if there is a local issue – either positive or negative – around which people can rally that can produce a good outcome. For example, can the road widening scheme be stopped or the pelican crossing built or the local school open its doors to evening meetings etc?

It is difficult, though possible, for volunteers to achieve such outcomes, then turn support and enthusiasm into a lasting organisation, which aims to improve the whole neighbourhood. Two ways forward which make progress easier can be adopted. They can be tried separately or together:

1. If an employed Community Organiser does not already exist, one must be found and funded.

2. A Community Organiser can use a nearby recovered neighbourhood to show those just setting out on the path to recovery which steps to take. That is, if you need your neighbourhood improving and want to start a Forum, go to someone who knows how to do it because they have already done it.

A Neighbourhood Forum can take different forms. It might take the form of an open meeting once every month or two. Or, the open meeting might elect or choose a committee of a dozen or so people to represent them between the open meetings.

The active people can get training in the skills needed to Chair meetings, take minutes and employ people. Voluntary work can be fun and satisfying. It can also make people employable as well as improving their neighbourhood. Being a Community Organiser is about to become a 'growth industry'.

Once a Forum is up and running the Community Organiser and their Forum will want to do the following:

- Decide whether to register it as a Charity, Company Limited by Guarantee or turn it into a Development Trust. For, none of these need carry any personal financial liability.
- Help it to prepare an Action Plan or a Neighbourhood Development Plan.
- Set out to achieve some of the aims of residents fairly quickly so that people can see that you mean business.
- Make sure the Forum continues to become ever more widely reflective of all interests in the neighbourhood or people will say: "You are not representative."

Above all, the Community and members of the Forum will need to introduce people to each other and help them to feel part of a wider group of friends. To help them to achieve things together figure out how residents can achieve one or more of the following:

- Feel safer.
- Reduce anti-social behaviour.
- Make their street tidier.

- Make their street more attractive.
- Remove that car and graffiti which everyone hates
- Cultivate the confused space.
- Simply enjoy each others company and eat together.

In place of grand top-down projects which are here today and gone tomorrow, start with the little things. They will lead residents on to larger tasks which they once felt could not be tackled. But, remember, Rome was not built in a day!

A School for Social Entrepreneurs, a Residents Academy

Community Organisers and Active Citizens need help and resources to discover the courage of their convictions and to move obstacles aside so that they can build an agenda for local action and encourage the inclusion of the many not the few.

This will not be easy. Many have tried in the past. Most have failed and given up. If success is to be gained this time and the habit of achieving it is to replace the one of failure, the help given must be real, tangible and appropriate.

We have noted that the few neighbourhoods which have bucked the trend and laid down the path to success have had special leaders with special qualities. So, it has to be asked: If so far only a few such people have come forward, how can 3000 arise to lead the 3000 plus despairing neighbourhoods of the land?

The task sounds too difficult? Not a bit of it. Remember that when Roger Bannister first ran the mile in under four minutes everyone said that nobody else would ever do so again. Yet, today most good athletes can do so – in part because the mental barrier was also broken and because we now have special training schools and coaches.

Consider also Christopher Columbus. Even his own crew doubted they would reach America or even that it existed. They nearly threw him overboard and turned around for home. Yet today, crossing the Atlantic is routine for ships and planes and a whole new subject of cartography and navigation is taught in Colleges and Universities.

So, in part, the need for successful Social Entrepreneurs, Active Citizens and Community Organisers who will guide their neighbourhoods along the path to success can be answered in this way: "Set up a School for Social Entrepreneurs or a Residents Academy." Call it what you will. But, the next generation of social leaders will find their path to success eased if they can mingle with, learn from and be guided by the last one in just the same way that we now have Sports Academies and Schools of Cartography which teach the Rogers and Christophers of today.

Should an Academy be just for residents? Residents who were previously passive need help to become active. So also, once 'doing' officers and councillors need help if they are to become 'enablers' and respond positively, not defensively, to active residents.

Steps en route to setting up a Residents Academy

There are several steps to be considered as we think about how to set up a Residents Academy in most urban areas.

- The first step is to <u>change the culture</u>, the way we think. We must accept the fact that the values and social bonds which tie people together are now too weak to sustain decent standards and mutual support. Why has this happened and how can we remedy it?
- A second step forward is to devise and implement a <u>phased Rolling Programme of Recovering Neighbourhoods</u>. Surely the Academy will include more and more residents in more and more recovering neighbourhoods and provide them with the experience of success.
- However, on their own, culture change and a Rolling Programme are insufficient. Very few people have travelled the journey to sustainable recovery, understand where the elephant traps are or where the bridges and stepping stones are to be found. But, some have. Use them as guides.
- If we are not smart, we will ignore their experience and knowledge and ask each new set of Active Citizens and their Community Organisers to re-invent the wheel and set out on the journey of recovery without a route map or the guiding hand of those who have been there already.
- If, however, we are wise we will lend the wheel to others and connect the inexperienced traveller to the experienced one. In making this connection, we open the door to a Residents Academy in every urban authority.

What will a Residents Academy look like?

It does not need substantial premises, just a base for a library of books, videos, pamphlets, tool kits, an office and a meeting room. For, much of the school will be based out in those neighbourhoods where experienced residents who can act as tutors are to be found. So, the Academy doesn't need many staff. For, most of the tutors are dispersed and at work as voluntary Active Citizens in their own neighbourhoods. They are part-time tutors who are able to teach others in the way that the master craftsman teaches the apprentice – on the job, by learning through doing techniques.

At least initially, just one person and an assistant are sufficient to co-ordinate and sustain the work of the Academy. But, they will need to be in touch with as many experienced residents as they can find.

The Coordinator will need a variety of aids to hand. They will include:

- A list of experienced resident tutors who will be inducted and accredited either by the coordinator or by Senior Guides identified in leading Neighbourhoods.
- The tutors will each have a 'treasure trail' of people and places to visit which leads to confidence and recovery.

So at first, the Residents Academy really will be less of a physical entity and more of a federation or network of shared learning experiences in which those who are untutored team up with experienced Guides to staff the Rolling Programme of Flourishing Neighbourhoods and kick start the process of renewal, which will eventually include most troubled neighbourhoods.

As time goes on, the Academy will wish to consider how it can boost and inform the following:

- The teaching of Citizenship in Schools.
- The way young people can volunteer to make a contribution to the community in a kind of gap year in the community.
- How Active Citizens can be honoured in their neighbourhood and city and become role models.
- How senior Social and Civic Entrepreneurs can move on to gain a Masters in the subject at a College or University.

Just as Universities noted the achievement of Christopher Columbus and asked their Schools of Geography to expand to teach cartography and re-draw the atlas, so also it is time for them to re-draw the social map and add practical courses for social leaders. Whilst some of these will no doubt entail chalk and talk, the best will rely on 'learning through doing' and 'seeing is believing' techniques out in neighbourhoods.

It is salutary to recall that Ruskin College was set up in Oxford to cater for and advance the new role of 'Shop Steward' and 'Trades Unionist'. Similarly, Sidney and Beatrice Webb founded the London School of Economics to teach the Social Sciences to those who they hoped would staff the Welfare State. Perhaps the time is ripe for a new Ruskin College for the Street Steward and Community Organiser, for Ted, Raja and Naseem. Shouldn't each University in each urban area consider how to support their local Residents Academy and dignify it with certificates and awards?

The next chapter emphasises one special feature in the make up of the Community Organiser and the Active Citizen. For, recall, unlike their statutory counterpart, they are not delivering a service so much as a new way of life which is driven by values and faith. The chapter then asks: "Can faith move mountains?" Just what effect can a good organiser and Active Citizens who have faith in each other have on the neighbourhood where they live and work?

Chapter 5

THE CRUCIAL ROLE OF FAITH –
CAN IT MOVE MOUNTAINS?

All the steps in the slow process of renewal described earlier, all the changed people who changed places and the work of the Community Organiser are bound together by ultimate values, by faith in each other and in the future. At first, few residents, let alone policy-makers realised this. But, the penny slowly dropped in Balsall Heath, especially at the sight of Muslim and Christian volunteers with their sleeves rolled up reclaiming the wildly overgrown garden of a Council House in which lived a lone 85 year old lady who could neither use it nor tend it.

An encounter between a journalist from a national newspaper and a dozen Balsall Heath residents is telling. He was trying to get them to confess that they resented all the volunteering work they had to do to improve their neighbourhood, that they objected to the fact that the Council did not do it for them and that they would far rather be at home watching TV. It took him a while to understand and accept what they were saying, which in summary form was this: "But, we enjoy it. We make new friends. People say 'thank you'. People respect you. It makes you feel proud and good."

Faith, as they say, can move mountains. It does so by binding people together and giving them the strength not just of numbers but of conviction and belief. One important milestone in the journey of Balsall Heathans was when a group of Muslim volunteers lead by Abdullah, the Community Organiser, gently chided some members of the local Christian Church:

In November 2002, Abdullah said: "You don't assert your faith enough. You are too timid. You don't even go Carol singing any more at Christmas. Tell you what," he said: "We Muslims will go Carol singing this year. Join in if you like."

Of course, the Christians did so and enjoyed it. So too did the residents who lived in the streets in which they sang and the elders in the sheltered accommodation they visited. Ever since, the Muslims, Sikhs and Christians have jointly collected the food hampers described earlier and delivered them at Christmas and at Eid. The communal meals attended by 300 residents are another manifestation of faith. As they say, the family which eats together stays together.

Faith is not normally a part of the language of the politician. It is regarded as being in the province of the Priest and Friday or Sunday prayers. But, in the case of Balsall Heath, it is used everyday to motivate and care for the community. It has moved mountains of problems and replaced them with a desirable community and village to live in.

In this sense, those Muslims from Pakistan who settled in depressed and deprived Balsall Heath have not just shown Christians how to rejoice in singing carols again. They have also shown the Big State how it needs to change its role to that of an 'Enabling' one which commissions fewer services and encourages and invests in faith and Community Organisers who can save it and the taxpayers large sums of money. For, prevention really is far better and cheaper than expensive cure.

Can the State hear the message from Balsall Heath about the vital role of faith in renewal and replicating it widely? Can it acknowledge and broadcast the fact that Muslim newcomers from Pakistan have helped to define that role and reminded Christians of its importance? Can it initiate and contribute to a prolonged national culture-changing debate in which the role of faith is placed at the very centre of social life?

Jonathan Sacks wrote 'The Politics of Hope' followed by 'The Home we build Together'. Amitai Etzioni and Robert Putnan published a series of riveting books in the last 20 years explaining why society had become too weak to support people and families and what had to be done to strengthen it.

These profoundly important books show why the future of our neighbourhoods and society is not just dependent on politicians and the State but, even more importantly, on the community sector and ultimate values, faith. Their ability to provide us all with shared moral goals which give order and meaning to our lives has been demonstrated in a host of practical ways through the people and activities described above. That is, we don't just need good policies. We need good people driven by Faith, or faith. For, people do not need to belong to a particular Faith Agency to be driven by faith in each other and in the common good.

The Statistics of success – the power of faith

It is time to ask: "Where did all these little, faltering, steps lead?" Just what is the outcome of all these changed people and places?" "What is the mountain which Faith has moved in Balsall Heath?" Remember for a moment, that 30 years ago Balsall Heath had been Birmingham's least desirable neighbourhood for some time. It was infested with crime and grime. People had arrived to live there from the 4 corners of the World and did not know each other. The providers of statutory services told them to move if they could for there was nothing which they, with all their budgets, could do.

A couple of years ago Birmingham's Strategic Partnership commissioned an opinion poll and asked 8,070 people from all over Birmingham these questions: Do you feel safe in your neighbourhood, are you satisfied by it, can you influence events in it and do you trust people in it? These are the results of that survey.

Percentage who thought most people in the area could be trusted

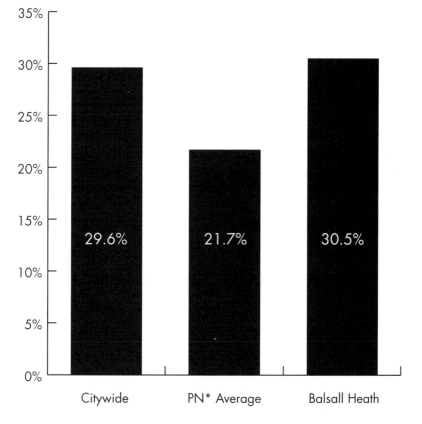

*PN = Priority Neighbourhood

Percentage who feel they can influence decisions in their locality

% Agree they can influence decisions

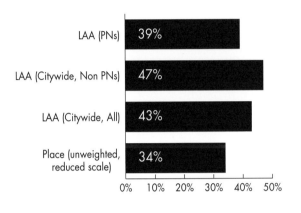

LAA (PNs)	39%
LAA (Citywide, Non PNs)	47%
LAA (Citywide, All)	43%
Place (unweighted, reduced scale)	34%

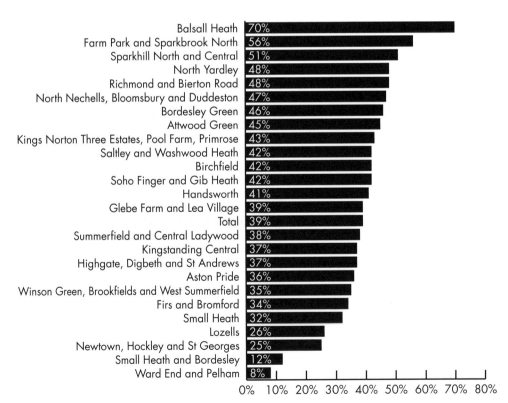

Balsall Heath	70%
Farm Park and Sparkbrook North	56%
Sparkhill North and Central	51%
North Yardley	48%
Richmond and Bierton Road	48%
North Nechells, Bloomsbury and Duddeston	47%
Bordesley Green	46%
Attwood Green	45%
Kings Norton Three Estates, Pool Farm, Primrose	43%
Saltley and Washwood Heath	42%
Birchfield	42%
Soho Finger and Gib Heath	42%
Handsworth	41%
Glebe Farm and Lea Village	39%
Total	39%
Summerfield and Central Ladywood	38%
Kingstanding Central	37%
Highgate, Digbeth and St Andrews	37%
Aston Pride	36%
Winson Green, Brookfields and West Summerfield	35%
Firs and Bromford	34%
Small Heath	32%
Lozells	26%
Newtown, Hockley and St Georges	25%
Small Heath and Bordesley	12%
Ward End and Pelham	8%

Percentage satisfied with the local area

% satisfied with local area

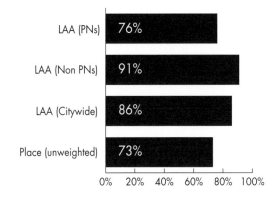

LAA (PNs)	76%
LAA (Non PNs)	91%
LAA (Citywide)	86%
Place (unweighted)	73%

0% 20% 40% 60% 80% 100%

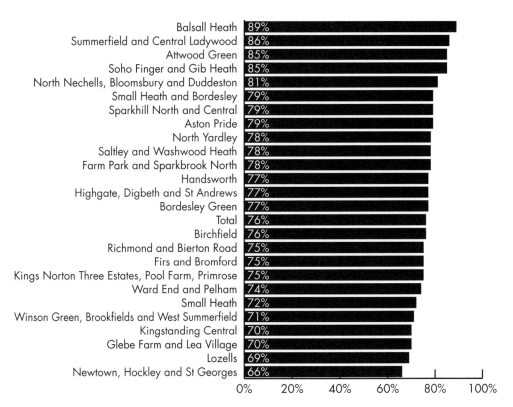

Balsall Heath	89%
Summerfield and Central Ladywood	86%
Attwood Green	85%
Soho Finger and Gib Heath	85%
North Nechells, Bloomsbury and Duddeston	81%
Small Heath and Bordesley	79%
Sparkhill North and Central	79%
Aston Pride	79%
North Yardley	78%
Saltley and Washwood Heath	78%
Farm Park and Sparkbrook North	78%
Handsworth	77%
Highgate, Digbeth and St Andrews	77%
Bordesley Green	77%
Total	76%
Birchfield	76%
Richmond and Bierton Road	75%
Firs and Bromford	75%
Kings Norton Three Estates, Pool Farm, Primrose	75%
Ward End and Pelham	74%
Small Heath	72%
Winson Green, Brookfields and West Summerfield	71%
Kingstanding Central	70%
Glebe Farm and Lea Village	70%
Lozells	69%
Newtown, Hockley and St Georges	66%

0% 20% 40% 60% 80% 100%

Percentage feeling safe in the local area

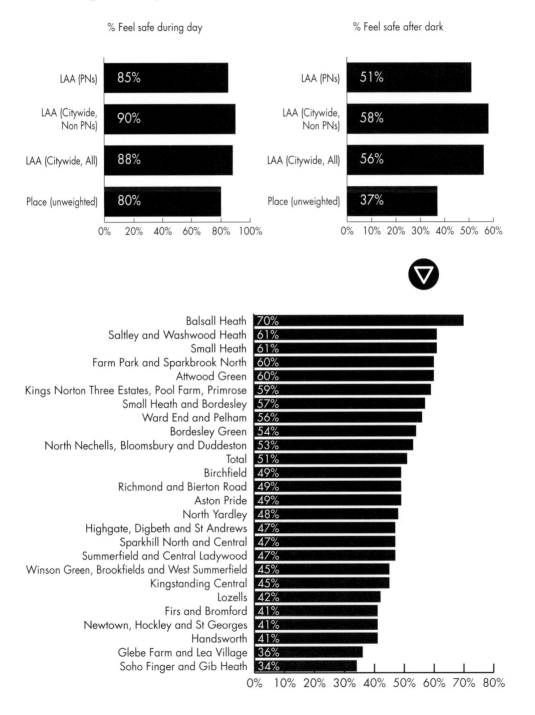

% Feel safe during day

LAA (PNs)	85%
LAA (Citywide, Non PNs)	90%
LAA (Citywide, All)	88%
Place (unweighted)	80%

% Feel safe after dark

LAA (PNs)	51%
LAA (Citywide, Non PNs)	58%
LAA (Citywide, All)	56%
Place (unweighted)	37%

Balsall Heath	70%
Saltley and Washwood Heath	61%
Small Heath	61%
Farm Park and Sparkbrook North	60%
Attwood Green	60%
Kings Norton Three Estates, Pool Farm, Primrose	59%
Small Heath and Bordesley	57%
Ward End and Pelham	56%
Bordesley Green	54%
North Nechells, Bloomsbury and Duddeston	53%
Total	51%
Birchfield	49%
Richmond and Bierton Road	49%
Aston Pride	49%
North Yardley	48%
Highgate, Digbeth and St Andrews	47%
Sparkhill North and Central	47%
Summerfield and Central Ladywood	47%
Winson Green, Brookfields and West Summerfield	45%
Kingstanding Central	45%
Lozells	42%
Firs and Bromford	41%
Newtown, Hockley and St Georges	41%
Handsworth	41%
Glebe Farm and Lea Village	36%
Soho Finger and Gib Heath	34%

What next? money and management

I rest my case that faith really can motivate people to move mountains. It's taken a generation, but in that generation the above statistics show that Balsall Heath has moved from being at the bottom of the class to being at the top of it. That's a dramatic change. However, it's not unique. Scattered throughout the land are a limited number of other neighbourhoods which have undergone a similar transformation. Good news! The most recent surveys in Birmingham show that other neighbourhoods are catching up with Balsall Heath. Some are even overtaking it.

Just take this additional fact from Castle Vale, an outer ring council housing estate. Twenty years ago it ran Balsall Heath a close second to the title 'the least desirable neighbourhood in Birmingham'. Just a dozen years ago its public housing stock was given to its residents to manage. They not only improved the look and feel of their houses, they transformed their social environment. Just 10 years ago residents in Castle Vale died 8 years sooner than the Birmingham average. Today, they die just 2 years sooner. That is, in 10 years they have come to live 6 years longer. That's special. That's a real mountain moved.

Are there other services which can be managed more cost effectively? The implications for the way we have organised services and budgets are immense. Consider this: If the bottom-up, faith driven, transformation of Balsall Heath can move mountains of statistics and enable people to live happier, healthier, safer, lives does it also save money? Is the prevention of ills not just better than letting them arise and then curing them, is it also cheaper?

We have pointed out that residents, not the Police, prevented the practice of prostitution. The Police were then able to disband their vice squad which had cost £350k per year. That was 12 years ago and 12 x 350 = £4.2m, quite a saving. When you add to this sum the costs the courts saved in sentencing prostitutes and other criminals, the Fire Service saved not having to attend so many fires, social services saved because fewer elderly people were taken into institutional care, then the figure becomes very large indeed. We have to conclude that 'prevention really is better and cheaper than cure', moreover it means that the bottom-up empowerment of residents does 'more for less' than the existing top-down way of organising care in our society.

A new role for the residents means a new role for the State

It is now time to ask this question: If that's what residents can do for each other from the bottom-up, what are the implications of this for top-down service providers, for the State? Does it, should it, change?

The new and developing role described above for the Active Resident and Community Organiser and their dramatic success has major implications for the way we see the individual in relation to the State and the political system.

The extension of the franchise 100 years ago meant that all people over the age of 21 gained the vote. Instead of rule by unelected Lords or just an elite, this meant that everyone could now have a say in who governs them. But, great advance though this was, the vote was confined to a once a year act in Council elections and every 5 years in National ones. For the other 364 or 364x5 days Government was confined to the few who were elected and the State and local bureaucracies which these few managed, which delivered services 'to' people.

This huge advance in democracy has resulted in many benefits. Our world is far better for it and many around the world now seek to emulate that. However, we have discovered that there has also been a real down-side to the franchise. It has resulted in a 'doing' State which provides things 'for' people and only asks them to participate once every 1 or 5 years. It has inadvertently developed structures, budgets and a culture which have made people dependent and inactive. The once hallowed vote, which residents chained themselves to railings to gain, has fallen dramatically. Residents now complain that politics and the State are not delivering the goods and that they have to do it themselves. So, what are the implications for the State of the everyday empowerment of residents in Balsall Heath and their statistics of success? Can the State develop a new role, which doesn't just acknowledge people once every 1 or 5 years but which empowers people every day especially at Neighbourhood level? If so, what changes will the State have to make in the way it provides services and money for neighbourhoods? The next chapter starts to answer these questions.

Chapter 6

CHANGING THE TOP-DOWN

Background

At first Balsall Heath's Active Residents, Community Organiser and Forum did not realise the radical implications for their Partners of their common sense actions to improve the living conditions, which their Statutory Partners had told them was not possible. They simply got on with the practical job of helping each other to care for their neighbourhood. But, as time went on and the village became more and more robust, residents began to ask: "Will our Partners now adjust their services to suit the new, changed, circumstances of the neighbourhood and to meet our needs?"

They reflected on the fact that they could influence and improve the product on offer in the private sector's high street with the purchasing power of their purse. But, although they were the customer, paid taxes and voted, they were not only unable to influence what was on offer in the public sector's back street where they lived, they did not even know what the tax-payer's budget for their neighbourhood was, nor who was managing it.

So, they asked: "What is the budget for our neighbourhood?" They soon found out that nobody, not even Councillors or Senior Officers knew what their neighbourhood cost. Their neighbourhood had no manager, no neighbourhood development or business plan and no budget. For, these were inextricably subsumed within the budgets and one-size-fits-all plans covering far larger areas, which contained very many administratively indistinguishable neighbourhoods. In this sense, whole neighbourhoods are 'confused' spaces. One Trades Unionist said: "If a business was organised like this it would have gone bust years ago and no Bank Manager would ever loan it money. So, why should we?" He concluded that the Balsall Heath Forum should appoint a Neighbourhood Manager to begin "to get a grip on things and to relate the public's top-down to the resident's bottom-up." Interestingly, the Trades Unionist soon joined hands with a couple of shopkeepers who were similarly astonished that those who received and distributed their taxes had no idea what the social business of Balsall Heath cost and that nobody was responsible for it.

It took the Community Organiser, the Trades Unionist and local business people a few years to come up with new solutions. But, Balsall Heath and a few other succeeding neighbourhoods now have:

- A Neighbourhood Manager
- A Neighbourhood Strategic Partnership of all the players
- A neighbourhood plan
- The beginnings of a neighbourhood budget

That is, the change in the role of the once passive resident who received top-down services from the State to that of active participant complete with Community Organiser and Neighbourhood Forum has dramatic implications for the way statutory services are delivered in future.

This chapter will describe the crucial developments which any self-respecting neighbourhood needs if it is to become well managed and respond to the needs and wishes of their newly active resident customer. But, first, it will be useful to picture the change in style and attitude which are involved:

The change from a Welfare State to a Welfare Society, from the Franchise to Empowerment

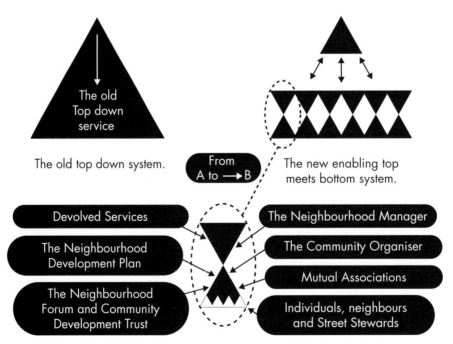

When the change from A to B is pictured in this way, you can see that it not only gives the public sector's customer and tax-payer the kind of role they play in the high street, it is also a little like moving from the monopoly of an Empire to the diversity of a Commonwealth of Nations or, rather, of neighbourhoods. This is a helpful analogy. For, it reminds us that few Empires ever gave up their monopoly easily. They resisted. So, if the public sector's move to a Commonwealth of Neighbourhoods is to be willingly accomplished, we will have to spell out in positive and convincing detail just how beneficial to everyone, including the State, the changes will be. Neighbourhood Management is where the future lies. But, getting there, moving from the culture of 'before' and 'doing' to the one of 'after' and 'enabling' will not be easy either for residents or professionals.

When you think about it, the real raison d'etre of Neighbourhood Management flows from the need to empower residents and use their energy and skills to drive civil and neighbourhood renewal. Because resident ownership leads to sustainable renewal, it is both common sense and practical reality to put neighbourhoods first. That's where residents live and have their being. It's from their troubled back streets and confused public spaces that an agenda for action forms, which gives rise to a Neighbourhood Development Plan. Delivering that plan demands that Statutory Partners disentangle themselves and their budgets from their top-down silos and rearrange them according to the needs of the residents, their customer. This is the logic and rationale of the Welfare Society.

For 100 years we have followed the quite different logic of the Welfare State. Far from focussing on the customer, it concentrated on the needs of the producer, the service delivered, their master, Representative Democracy. This meant focussing on a ward, most of which contain parts of at least 3 neighbourhoods with other wards containing other parts of them. The constituencies of MP's and Central Government invariably contain 3 or 4 Wards, that is a dozen or more neighbourhoods. Further, the administrative boundaries via which the producer delivered one-size-fits-all services often did not even coincide with ward or constituency boundaries but would subsume many of these. Thus, wards, constituencies and administrative boundaries were beyond the reach of all but the politically active. The vast majority of people – and their vision and energy – were excluded. The Welfare State supposed that this did not matter. For, residents were receivers of state benevolence, the collective contribution of the representative system, and not the active participant.

Sidney and Beatrice Webb's LSE, and schools of Social Studies up and down the land taught generation after generation of kindly, well intentioned, Officers this 'self-evident truth of collectivism' and inadvertently created the despairing urban deserts of today. This is precisely why a previous chapter of this book explained that today we need a quite different School, one for Social Activists and Community Organisers, a Residents Academy. This chapter explains the implications for tomorrow's service deliverers.

Fast forward 10 years: How far will devolution and empowerment have developed? What will the partnership between Active Citizens and a new enabling authority look like? How many of the nation's 3000 plus excluded neighbourhoods will have become strong and included?

When the Local Management of Schools (LMS) was introduced 20 years ago schools were given their independence. Few then realised what self-governing schools meant for the future of LEA's (Local Education Authorities). Today of course, we no longer have an LEA but a Children's Department. Further, many free schools will soon have even more autonomy and what was once the mighty LEA will be a small strategic part of that Children's Department. So, if not just schools but significant parts of other services and assets are also to pass to strong neighbourhoods and if Neighbourhood Management is to become the norm rather than the isolated exception, what will the public sector's central Council, its constituencies and wards look like in 2022?

The question will become less one of 'which bits and pieces of services should be delivered locally' and more 'which bits should not be delivered locally?' In 10 years time, in addition to schools, key parts if not all of such services as these could also be delivered locally within neighbourhoods:

- Representation.
- Neighbourhood policing.
- Public Housing.
- Parks.
- Environmental services.
- Care for the elderly and children.
- Public assets, land and buildings.
- Safety.
- Health.

Of course, we will still need a Chief Constable and specialist Police able to cover several if not many neighbourhoods, and while some environmental services can be local, not every neighbourhood can or should have its own refuse wagon and urban tip. But, it is likely that each neighbourhood will acquire its own dedicated inter-agency team of workers who will take pride in delivering a high-quality product.

It follows that the significance of the ward and constituency will dwindle as more and more people become involved in service delivery in their neighbourhood. That is, the constituency, like the central council and the LEA, will become less of a doer and more of an enabler which passes previously central services right down to grass-roots level. What are the neighbourhood's equivalents of moving from an LEA to a Children's Department?

So that Officers and Councillors can see more clearly where their future lies, it really is important to spell out a 10 plus year vision for devolution and neighbourhood empowerment. What will the enabling authority of 2022 look like? What is the neighbourhood likely to look like and how will the partnership between it and the State work? Until these questions are answered, many Officers and Councillors will view the transition with trepidation. So, we really do need to add an officer and Councillor dimension to our proposed Residents Academy

Introducing the Local Management of Neighbourhoods (LMN) is a logical extension of the Local Management of Schools (LMS)

It is worth recalling that the government of the day which introduced LMS did not give schools and local authorities a choice. It said: "You will all become LM within 5 years. In year one 'x' number of schools will start the process, in year two 'y' number will start and so on until they all are LM. You may find this difficult if left to your own devices. So, we will give Heads, new School Bursars, Governors and Chairs of Governors training and clear guidance about what we expect. And, we will create an Ofsted, put failing schools into special measures and not let them out until they can demonstrate success."

Had Local Authorities been given a choice about whether to become LM or not, we would still be waiting for LM schools to arrive. Had schools not been given training, they would have made so many mistakes that the process of transition would have been halted and put into reverse.

So, if we are to progress to LMN (Locally Managed Neighbourhoods), we are well advised to learn the lessons of the success of the LMS story. If we do this we will put the following into motion:

- Start a Rolling Programme of LMN neighbourhoods in each urban area.
- Weak and unconfident residents in each of these neighbourhoods will need the training and support of a Community Organiser and Residents Academy who will help them to become well organised and able to represent others fairly and inclusively.
- Similar capacity building will be needed by Officers and Councillors as they move from doing to enabling mode. Both new active residents and new enabling Officers/Councillors will need joint guidance in the arts and skills of Neighbourhood Management, Neighbourhood Planning, budgeting and the bending of mainstream budgets.
- Further, we will probably need our own home-grown neighbourhood version of an Ofsted, a kind of Ofsthood which identifies and puts failing neighbourhoods into special measures and requires them to be placed under 'new management'.
- Finally, we will also need a Code of Conduct which resident representatives and officers sign up to which outlines the kind of conduct which is and is not acceptable and distinguishes between the all inclusive style of participatory democracy and the party politics of the public sector.

Unless we plan the transition from 'old' to 'new' in this way, we will, in effect, be encouraging people to make mistakes, get things horribly wrong and invite those who seek to preserve the status quo to say: "See, look at that bad behaviour. I told you that we couldn't trust residents. Stop the process. Stay as we are".

So, the sections of the chapter that follow spell out the key features of Neighbourhood Management.

Neighbourhood Management

The foundation stones required for Neighbourhood Management include:

- The geographically defined neighbourhood itself.
- Community ownership, the Capacity Organiser and Forum.
- Reopening top-down services under the new management of a Senior Neighbourhood Officer and their inter-departmental Neighbourhood Team.
- A Neighbourhood Area Agreement or Development Plan to be delivered by the Neighbourhood Team.
- A neighbourhood budget.
- Those driving both top-down and bottom-up coming to act as confident community and Statutory Partners.

Neighbourhoods

The first remedial task to undertake is to enable local people to gather together and define the area in which they live, much like villages of old 'beat their bounds'. How can revitalised communities be given an outward expression? How can the many urban villages from which each town is built be excavated from beneath the accumulated concrete and administrative jungle and exert their identity upon the physical, social and economic geography of tomorrow? How can a drab neighbourhood, a collection of confused spaces, be turned into a place which people own and of which they are proud? The following suggestions form only a brief introductory answer which might begin to name and assert the sense of place and identity of each neighbourhood or urban village.

As the charity Common Ground has shown, urban villages need to mark their boundaries with clear entry and exit signs. There is sense in making these obvious and distinctive, like postal district signs so that residents and visitors can know when they are being 'welcomed' within these boundaries or invited to return upon leaving. They also need a central focal point. It does not matter whether shops, a library, school or community centre identify the centre as long as it is clear to residents where this centre is, and that it has the right atmosphere whether because of its architecture or the quality of the services which it offers (or both). Perhaps a distinctive flag, crest or shield might help to give identity to both the entry gateways and the central features of the village.

At Christmas, Diwali, Eid, carnival time or during some other local celebrations, both gateways and central features might be enhanced by festive decorations, perhaps prepared by schools, religious organisations, residents groups or other voluntary organisations. The content and style of the celebration will of course vary, but no matter what the content these are important occasions and the more people who take part in the planning and execution of them the better. Such occasions can represent the strength of the community in a variety of forms including sport, art and business as well as being purely social or religious events. They can serve to highlight calendar festivals and mark the natural passing of the seasons which urban life otherwise obscures.

The neighbourhood needs a Manger

You might think it is surprising that up to now we did not know what the budget of each neighbourhood was. But, it is even more of a shock to realise that we did not have a development plan which explained how that money would be spent. Further, until very recently no neighbourhood had a Neighbourhood Manager who was responsible for the quality of services delivered or who was accountable for the large sums of public money they cost – or for the maintenance and strategic use of public assets, buildings and land.

It is important to press the point. To continue our analogy with schools, if schools were run in the way neighbourhoods are run, they would have:

- No visible budget.
- Nobody to account for the budget.
- No development plan for spending that budget or improving standards.
- No Head Teacher and certainly, no Governing Body.

Just how did we devise such a peculiar way of looking after such large sums of money and why have we not questioned it for so long? Better late than never. We can now see that in addition to a Community Organiser and Neighbourhood Forum each troubled neighbourhood also needs a senior Neighbourhood Manager who will be responsible for ensuring that top-down services are joined up and directed at the targets set by a Neighbourhood Development Plan.

Put another way, it's as if a neighbourhood had not just become a confused assembly of confused physical spaces, it had also become a confused social space. Not only had people forgotten who owned the physical fabric of it, they had also lost ownership and control of its social fabric.

A Neighbourhood Manager is needed to help the Forum and its partners to remedy this major defect. The Manager might be appointed or seconded from the ranks of local authority officers or they might come from outside the local authority. Indeed, it is important that many come from industry, the Police or health professions to whom they will have to relate just as directly as any local authority department. Alternatively, they could be from the voluntary sector.

It is important to remember that 3,000 plus of these senior managers will eventually be needed, one for each excluded neighbourhood. It will not be easy to identify, recruit, train and support so many, especially as they will have to be independent spirits able to rise to daunting challenges and to manage themselves as well as their inner-agency Neighbourhood Team. Someone who was previously trapped and frustrated within the Local Authority may surprise us all. Equally, someone who was experienced in setting-up and running the new branch of an expanding business may have a head start. Either way, they too will benefit from being able to use the Residents Academy.

Crucially, the Senior Manager will need to think in new ways, bang established heads together, assemble an inter-agency team of players able to help the Community Organiser and Forum to deliver the Neighbourhood Development Plan, meet and improve upon ambitious targets. So, the Neighbourhood Manager of statutory services will wish to:

- Work closely with his/her Community Organiser counterpart. Together, they are the flip sides of the coin of Neighbourhood Management.
- Bring all Statutory Partners together with the Forum in a Neighbourhood Strategic Partnership.
- Emerge a local team of all the players to work on joined up problems and devise solutions.
- Assist the Forum and all Statutory Partners with the annual preparation and review of the Neighbourhood Development Plan.
- Ensure that the statutory components and targets of that plan are hit and improved upon via the work of the neighbourhood team.
- Be responsible for the devolved budget of the neighbourhood and use it to drive the neighbourhood plan.
- Enable the Community's Organiser and local associations to trade with devolved statutory services and, where appropriate, undertake some of these services.
- Help the Local Authority to move from a situation where the community sector is dependent on time-limited grants and regeneration initiatives to one where it is invested in via detached parts of mainstream budgets.

At first, the Neighbourhood Strategic Partnership may well help existing specialist service providers to improve the quality of that provision. By degrees, however, a number of these services may be passed to the community to deliver and, beyond that, some services will be rendered redundant because the community is able to fend for and support itself and prevent major problems from arising.

The Cost? Not a lot:

Community Organiser	£25k
Neighbourhood Manager	£35k
Running costs	£10k
	£70k

Where will the money come from? We showed earlier how the Community Organiser can be funded. The Manager can easily be funded in the same way by money which is saved via prevention. Just 5 burglaries prevented, or one elderly person kept at home and out of care would suffice.

The Neighbourhood Strategic Partnership (NSP) and Neighbourhood Team

Specialist services have been delivered in top-down, one-size-fits-all ways via institutional silos over large tracts of land. But, the resident customer and their Forum need representatives from these specialisms to meet together and play to each other's strengths and support them where they are weak. So, each Partner needs to identify a person who will join a Neighbourhood Strategic Partnership (NSP), relax out of their silos and see how their services can become more joined up. For, the problems and possibilities which the resident customer identifies do not fit neatly into specialisms. For example, dealing with crime is not just a matter for the police. It is also affected by housing, social services, environmental and educational issues.

Whilst the NSP of Partners will wish to meet and consider joint action, say, every month, the joint action which follows will need to take place every week, if not every day. So, Partners will also need to identify at least one existing colleague who can be seconded to join a devolved Neighbourhood Team under the supervision and co-ordination of the Neighbourhood Manager. Of course, the Joint Team will need a joint base. A later chapter considers where this base might be and what it will look like.

The Neighbourhood Development Plan

No self-respecting business in the private sector would dream of trading without the guidance of a Business Development Plan. And no self-respecting banker would lend a business money unless they had studied the plan and verified that it was realistic. Recently, school managers have discovered the need for each school to have a School Development Plan which reviews progress and targets on a year-on-year basis.

It is common sense as well as good business practice for each neighbourhood's NSP and joint Neighbourhood Team to work out a Neighbourhood Development Plan or its residents and the agencies which service them will not know what targets they are aiming to achieve, whether they are falling short or improving, what they are costing or if they are worth it.

Each strong Neighbourhood Manager and Community Organiser will want their Neighbourhood Development Plan to be ambitious and aim to help to turn the whole area around within, say, five years and then sustain progress. It will need to address all of the following subjects and set ambitious targets for achieving progress:

- *Defining the neighbourhood.* Drawing the boundary of the neighbourhood in social and communal and not planning terms suggests the need to reorder political, council departments, Police and other administrative areas. Lines should be re-drawn to conform with that boundary – no easy task. The process may take 2 or 3 years before it is complete. But, it is an essential first step before the Boundary Commissioners come to play their part. For, it is their task to agree local ward and parliamentary, boundaries and, long term, it is sensible for these to reinforce the identity of neighbourhoods.
- *The family* is the basis of the community and the living springboard from which the child leaps into maturity and independence. Families which are not fortunate enough to have more than one voice and one pair of hands, who cannot benefit from the wisdom of uncles, aunts and grandparents can be substantially helped by neighbours and more experienced parents. Schemes like Sure Start help to organise mature parents to assist those who are disorganised and risk giving inconsistent and contradictory messages to their impressionable children.
- *Good physical and mental health* is essential if the family is to be cared for and the individual to be economically and socially self-reliant and benefit from, as well as contribute to, a spirited communal life. Prevention is better than cure. Yet, the disproportionately high child death rate, the death of adults from heart disease etc, causes both an economic and emotional drain on the typical troubled neighbourhood. Alongside the medical practice and hospital bed, adequate care in the community measures and a healthy living centre are needed to encourage people to lead a healthier, more robust, life-style.
- *The house or flat* needs to be bright, secure, have a front door which is personal and private and have an entry way and private or shared garden which is attractive and generates pride. Private ownership contributes to a thriving family life. When ownership is public or shared individuals should be able to become personally involved and influence the way their property is managed. Priority Estates Planning and others have pioneered tenant management of tower and low-rise blocks. They illustrate the many benefits seen by tenants managing their own housing stock.

- *The School* boosts or blights the child's life chances as much as the child's family does.
- *Employment* both engenders dignity and provides the individual with the ability to support themselves and their dependants. It enables the individual not to be a drain on finances, but to pay taxes which help both the Exchequer and those who have fallen on hard times. Good schooling and training is one answer. So also is work experience and the creation of Community Enterprises. Manufacturing industries will continue to shrink and technology alone cannot sustain high/full employment. In future, the service industries will continue to grow as will the need to care for an ever-increasing elderly population. The third sector is a growth industry whose job creation potential is yet to be fully explored.
- *Community safety* is a key to improving the quality of life. Of course, conventional arrests must be encouraged but, as innovative schemes like restorative justice and Neighbourhood Wardens illustrate, community involvement and preventative policing can reduce crime dramatically and make the delivery of other aspects of this Neighbourhood Plan much easier.
- *The built and green environment* gives an enduring impression to the growing child and can, when properly stewarded, lift the spirit of the adult. It should go without saying that the building, park or gutter which is 'owned' by a local individual or agency or Forum will be maintained. How can the physical features of a neighbourhood be made to complement and boost the social ones?
- *Diverse Mutual Community Associations and Enterprises* will be created in all the arenas of neighbourhood life described above. Some of these will be purely voluntary, some will employ staff and, therefore, create jobs. Others, perhaps one or two per neighbourhood, will be sophisticated Community Trusts with a significant financial turnover. These will trade with and relate to self-governing statutory agencies – schools, housing associations, etc.

Alone, each of these distinctive features of the plan is not sufficient to achieve sustainable change. It is crucial that they are all tackled and managed together as vital parts of an integrated whole.

Quality Review and Inspection. All the above activities and targets should, as with any development plan, be reviewed on a year-on-year basis and updated accordingly. Residents and all agencies will wish to praise those who ensure that standards are set and achieved, to intervene where they are not and to reward where they are exceeded. Good practice should be disseminated from neighbourhood to neighbourhood and from Authority to Authority with the help of the Residents Academy. It is possible to summarise and illustrate the features of a Neighbourhood Plan in the form of a chart:

Chart of Neighbourhood Development Plan

Area	Key Players	Target	Review Date
The Family	All relevant agencies and key resident representatives	Help, say, 100 families. Create parent centres in every primary school	12 months
Health	All relevant agencies and key resident representatives	Reduce infant mortality by 20%. Set up Healthy Living Centres	12 months
The House	All relevant agencies and key resident representatives	Involve all tenants in the management of the house	12 months
The School	All relevant agencies and key resident representatives	Improve standards by 30%. Cluster and pool resources	12 months
Employment	All relevant agencies and key resident representatives	Reduce unemployment by 50%	Every 3 months
Crime	All relevant agencies and key resident representatives	Reduce crime by 50%	Every 3 months
The Environment	All relevant agencies and key resident representatives	Clear the litter, remove the graffiti	Every 3 months
Mutual Associations	All relevant agencies and key resident representatives	Enable all the residents to help each other at a very local level	12 months
Assets	All relevant agencies and key resident representatives	Take ownership of key parks, lands and buildings	12 months
Neighbourhood Management	All relevant agencies and key resident representatives	All key agencies to be actively involved	Every 3 months
Partnership between residents and statutory agencies	All relevant agencies and key resident representatives	The bottom-up and top-down to be playing fully to each others strengths	12 months
Quality review and inspection	All relevant agencies and key resident representatives	Set new plans and targets in 1 years time. Identify strengths and weaknesses	12 months

If the ambitious targets in each neighbourhood's plan are achieved then, in a few short years, it should be possible to turn a failing area around in just the same way we now know a failing school can be saved. All that is required is:

- Empowered residents.
- Good management by one Neighbourhood Manager and a joint NSP and Team.
- Clear sighted aims and targets.
- Enthusiasm.
- Inspection, sanction and praise by the NSP and resident's Forum.
- Perhaps later years and later stages of the Neighbourhood Development Plan will take in the ownership and management of real assets by local people. This will include land, buildings and, above all, the employment of local people.
- A budget.
- When and if this advanced stage is reached some Neighbourhood Forums, Associations, Enterprises and Trusts may well themselves take on the delivery of such key services as:
- Care in the community.
- Some other Social Services such as elderly day care.
- Some leisure services.
- Housing.
- Environmental works.
- Community enterprises and job creation.
- Swimming baths, libraries and parks.

The neighbourhood budget – and the neighbourhood Bursar or Treasurer

The Government of the day asked the Civil Service in the early 1980's what a school cost. It wondered if each school's budget could be passed to it and whether schools could be locally managed (LM). At first, the officials did not understand the question. They answered in terms of hundreds of pounds and referred to dinner money and jumble sales. The Government persisted. It asked what the school's buildings and teachers cost, the full budget. At the time, of course, this was invisibly consumed within the Local Education Authority's (LEA) budget. It managed all schools, none of which had their own budget or even knew what it was.

Finally, the question was answered properly. We now know that a typical primary can cost £2m and a secondary £3m or more. Further, each school now has 90% of this budget. In place of a remote LEA taking top-down one-size-fits-all decisions on behalf of all schools, each school takes it own particular decision about just how much to spend on chalk, computers, books, teachers etc – and they are much better for it. In place of just 10 Councillors elected via Wards controlling the way civil servants managed schools, now 10 ordinary people sit on the Governing body of each school. In a Local Authority area of, say, 200 schools, that is 3,000 people who are involved in place of just 15. That's subsidiarity! It's also empowerment.

When the question about 'what does a neighbourhood cost' was first posed, officials responded in a similar way to the way educational officials first answered the same question about schools. Nobody knew, because the different bits and pieces of what a neighbourhood cost were absorbed within the far wider budgets of the statutory silos of Police, health and local authority departments.

However, when each neighbourhood's fraction of these huge, far wider, statutory budgets is detached, we now know that it adds up to a staggering £100,000,000 plus, per year per neighbourhood of 15,000 people.

Yet to date, this sum has been invisible. It has been a confused financial space. It does not exist in practice and, therefore, nobody has been accountable for it. It is very important to make it visible and to disentangle it from the wider budgets of each statutory agency. Of course, some of it will always have to relate back to the far wider administrative area from which we have just theoretically detached it. Some bits and pieces can't be delegated to the neighbourhood's level of subsidiarity. For example, there can only be one Chief Constable, one University, one General Hospital, etc. So, some of the neighbourhood's sum has to be retained centrally to pay for them. When this top slicing has taken place, what fraction of the £100,000,000 can be devolved to each neighbourhood? Is it the 90% which schools now get, leaving the Chief Education's Officer with just 10%. Or, does rather more have to be retained?

Let's suppose that 50% has to be retained, at least to start with. That leaves £50,000,000 which can be devolved to neighbourhood level. Now, of course, some of that is still fairly inflexible and spoken for. For example, each school will still wish to retain its budget and the cutting of the park's grass will still require the driving of the mowing machine.

So, for the sake of the argument, let's also suppose the most of the £50,000,000 will at first be relatively fixed, say, 90% of it. This leaves us with two important considerations:

1. First, the 90% or £45,000,000 which is delegated but 'relatively fixed' can be used in imaginative, slightly different, ways. For example. Instead of say, the 3 primary schools on the patch (total cost 3 x £2,000,000 = £6,000,000) all advertising separately for a new teacher, they might advertise jointly. They might pursue a common procurement policy and get the park mower to also mow their grass etc, etc.

   Other schools in other neighbourhoods might respond quite differently. One set might even create a Family Centre. The scope and implications are enormous and diverse.

2. Second, the remaining 10%, just 5% of the total neighbourhood budget, which can initially be used differently amounts to £5,000,000 for each and every year. Although it is at this stage a tiny percentage, it is an enormous sum which the neighbourhood could not previously access. It dwarfs all previous forms of top-down external grant aid. Even more important, it is not time-limited, but is available for the pursuit of the civil renewal agenda for each and every year and for each and every neighbourhood in the land. That bares repetition and emphasis as follows:

This sum of £5,000,000 can be found within existing budgets. It dwarfs even the largest external top up sums spent on renewal over the last 40 years. But, in place of 'more of the same' failing ways of spending it, our Neighbourhood Manager and Community Organiser will force us to spend it in ways which link with the places where people live. It engages their attention. It is owned and accountable. Consider the future. When the new managers of these sums have been at work for a few years they will find even more exciting ways of using the 'spoken for' £45,000,000 and ways of detaching more than 10% of it. 15% would give them £7,500,000 a year to further rebuild the social and physical fabric of the neighbourhood. That is, if we begin to manage neighbourhoods in this way we could give every neighbourhood in the country the kinds of sums we recently gave to just 39 NDC areas without troubling the taxpayer.

We can begin to see why it is important to de-confuse and extract the neighbourhood budget from far wider ones, apply the principle of subsidiarity and use it differently. It is surely also important to account for that budget and spend it with the help of a Neighbourhood Bursar or Treasurer.

The Government and opposition have become very interested in Social Enterprises which, with the help of a Social Entrepreneur, create social capital and a robust community, not just good services. We must go a step-further and begin to think about how we can run a whole neighbourhood as a Social Enterprise.

From Cure to Prevention

At a time of austerity and cuts it is particularly important to spell out one more vital implication of the strong neighbourhood village built by the Community Organiser and Neighbourhood Manager with a Neighbourhood Budget. They save and raise money. How?

We have been discussing two rather different ways of caring for each other, the long established way of the Welfare State and its Empire and the new way of the Community Organiser and the Commonwealth.

In times past, successive Governments have devised ever more expensive services which they have delivered to passive residents over large tracts of land which did not relate to the smaller neighbourhoods where people live. Providing people with public housing, health, safety, childcare and green environments was well intentioned. But, the process was expensive and many people in many neighbourhoods continued to live in poor social circumstances. Instead of changing the way services were delivered in order to tackle these poor circumstances successive Governments also devised expensive but time limited renewal initiatives. But, as they were time limited, progress ended when the grant ended because they did not alter the way existing service delivery budgets were spent.

In present times of austerity, not only are external grants not possible but, there is less to spend on existing services. So, there is a danger that fewer existing services are delivered and that with cuts, we get 'less for less'. If so, more problems will arise which will be expensive to solve in the future. This will either build up pressure to ease the cuts or make it more difficult to deliver the Big Society and renewed neighbourhoods.

Neighbourhood Budgeting provides an alternative way forward. If we are to achieve successful renewal and build the Big Society, as discussed in earlier chapters we need to concentrate less on expensive service "cures" and more on "prevention". For, if we can prevent crimes from occurring and people from becoming ill etc, we can save a very great deal of money, as there would be far fewer problems to cure. Remember, this approach entails focussing less on the delivery of services 'to' passive customers and more on enabling residents to become active and to care for each other by living socially richer lives, precisely what the active citizen, Forum and Community Organiser do. Just what is prevented and what does it save and, does prevention also raise money?

The value of prevention – money raised and saved

Money Raised

The chart shows the average price of a terraced house in B12, Balsall Heath and in Birmingham as a whole from April 2000 – April 2010 as an index of their respective April 2000 values.

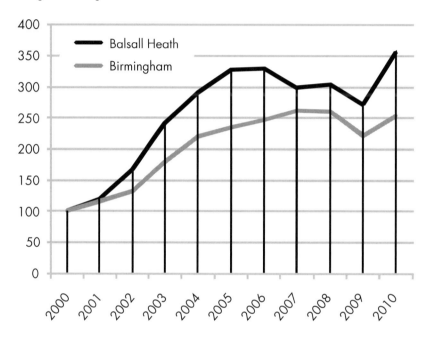

So, £1 invested in property in Balsall Heath in April 2000 was worth just over £3.50 in April 2010; whereas £1 invested in average Birmingham property was worth just £2.50 by April 2010. Even during the slump in property prices from early 2007 onwards, Balsall Heath stayed well ahead of the Birmingham average index.

Mean prices of terraced house sales taken from Land Registry data are shown opposite. They show that:

- 10 years ago, Balsall Heath prices were 20% below the Birmingham average.
- Today, they are 15% above it, a gain of 35% and of £105k per house.
- At today's prices, this represents a gain of £75m in value for public housing owners.
- The Forum needs just 0.1% of that to pay for its Community Organiser and Neighbourhood Manager!

Year	B12 average £	Birmingham average £
2000	40559	50867
2001	48346	58811
2002	68455	67215
2003	97967	91715
2004	117727	112369
2005	133245	120090
2006	133825	126071
2007	121444	133295
2008	123400	132432
2009	110750	113066
2010	145000	128968

So, creating a robust neighbourhood <u>raises</u> money. But, it also <u>saves</u> money.

Money saved

After retiring from the West Midland Police Force Dr Roger Patrick wrote a PhD thesis on Balsall Heath and showed how the dramatic fall in crime led to major savings in Police time, staffing and budgets. The Vice Squad cost £350k. As a result of residents action it was disbanded and £300k plus of other Officers were transferred out of the area due to a reduction in burglaries and other crimes. This saved a total of £650k/year.

The same savings need to be quantified for environmental, fire and other services. For example, Balsall Heath went from having the highest fire service call out figures in Birmingham to the lowest. A call-out costs £7k. If just 30 call-outs a year are saved this equals £210k.

Consider these possibilities for a typical neighbourhood like Balsall Heath:

Cost per event	Number of events prevented	Saving per year
1 murder costs £1m	3	£3m
1 elderly person in care costs £150k/year	15	£2.250m
1 burglary costs £14k	100	£1.4m
1 call out of the fire service costs £7k	100	£0.7m
1 teenage delinquent can cost £50k	20	£1m
1 Vice Squad	Not needed	£0.35m
Total spend which could be saved by prevention		£8,500,000

In the case of Balsall Heath, these factors also need to be taken into account:

- These are minimum figures. The real totals are higher. But, even as they stand, they show that per year, prevention can save 8.5% of the annual revenue cost of all services.
- If replicated in just 50 neighbourhoods in Birmingham this could save £425m/year!
- In sharp contrast, the annual cost of the Balsall Heath Forum which has triggered this outcome is just £300k. This is less than 3% of the savings made and only 0.3% of the cost of the whole neighbourhood. Yet, it could sustain renewal in the area for perpetuity.
- It is surely time to provide a finance expert or two to verify these figures and show how to save £8.5m/year/neighbourhood in return for an outlay of just 3% of that figure. Oh! And, to help us to decide what to do with the remaining 97% of these savings.

Just begin to imagine the national savings which could eventually be made if many neighbourhoods were all able to save £8.5m/year. As stated, if Birmingham can replicate this in 50 neighbourhoods, it equals £425m. If we can replicate it nationally in, say, 1000 neighbourhoods, that equals a saving of £21,250,000,000.

Once these savings are fully documented they should enable Balsall Heath's and other neighbourhood's Partners to see the real merits of the Big Society, invest in its sustenance and find no trouble at all in funding the Community Organiser and Neighbourhood Manager (£70k) which each neighbourhood needs to start the journey to recovery.

So, let's hear no more of cuts and 'less for less'. For, Neighbourhood Budgeting shows us how we can 'invest to save' and 'create more for less'. Surely, this has to be a constructive and very appealing alternative to simply cutting existing budgets and reducing services. The point bares emphasis. Empowered residents move mountains. They transform the quality of life in their neighbourhood. More, they open the door to:

Managing neighbourhoods more cost effectively. They:

- Raise money.
- Save money.
- Really do create 'more for less'.

The real value of a strong village, a good Community Organiser and a Neighbourhood Manager are becoming clear. They include:

- Producing a vibrant, spirited and supportive quality of life for residents.
- Enabling a new productive partnership (NSP) to arise between resident and State.
- The State moving from 'doing' to 'enabling'.
- Less money being spent by partners because of the problems which are prevented.
- New, joined-up services becoming targeted and neighbourhood specific.

So, the implications of a strong community and active citizens working from the bottom-up for the top-down services budgets and officers of the Welfare State are substantial. They are also impressive. They achieve far more in a neighbourhood strategic partnership with residents than they do from within their own silos. And, they save money in the process. So, it's worth looking in the next chapter in a little more detail at just what is entailed in Neighbourhood Budgeting and other forms of asset management and transfer.

Chapter 7

NEIGHBOURHOOD BUDGETING –
AND ASSET MANAGEMENT

There is even more to Neighbourhood Budgeting than first meets the eye. For, budgets need to be transformed, not just bent or top-sliced.

A friendly crime prevention Police Officer pointed out that his percentage of the Police budget was just 3% of the total. Thus, he said: "This means that 97% of it is spent on detecting criminals and getting them into court. Yet, only 3% is spent on preventing crime and avoiding all the costs of it."

He got quite excited. "This is daft", he said. "Spend 97% on catching a criminal but only 3% on stopping him. If I had 50% of the budget I could stop far more crime from happening. This would mean I'd need far fewer colleagues in uniform catching criminals." He shrugged. "I suppose that's why it won't change. Who would vote for fewer uniformed police?" But, when you think about it, maybe we should. It's not just the Police who should consider (1) top slicing their budget to fund the building of a strong village and prevent crime and (2) policing neighbourhoods with a far smaller budget because there is less crime. Consider the following:

- It's in the interest of the Doctor and Hospital to pay for:

  ▸ Smoking cessation.
  ▸ People to eat the proverbial apple a day.
  ▸ Walking not driving to the shop or school.

The Doctor would have fewer patients and would have more time to concentrate on prevention and the unavoidably sick.

- It's in the interest of the school and Local Authority Children's Departments to pay for:

- ► Parental involvement.
- ► Tackling children with difficulties at the earliest age, not when they have become so disruptive that they cost even more.
- ► Creating a better quality of life in the neighbourhood in which the school is embedded.

• It is in the interest of the Housing Department and Housing Associations to pay for:

- ► Welcome packs for new tenants.
- ► A person, perhaps a Neighbourhood Manager, who will join their services up at street and neighbourhood level.
- ► A shared person who will support tenants who struggle, a kind of surrogate Godparent or Grandma.

Environmental services, leisure and other services such as the benefits provided by the Ministry of Pensions and Works could and should all produce their own list, ask exactly the same question as the crime prevention Policeman and then act accordingly. When they do this, they really would be using key parts of their budget not to deliver a service but to invest in a safer, stronger, cleaner more confident and proud community.

Picturing the old and the new budget

It is possible to picture the re-engineering or re-distribution of the statutory services one-size-fits-all budget as follows:

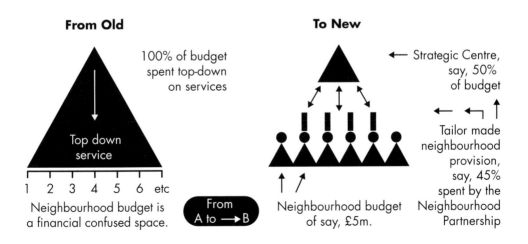

From Old

100% of budget
spent top-down
on services

Top down
service

1 2 3 4 5 6 etc

Neighbourhood budget is
a financial confused space.

From
A to ➝ B

To New

← Strategic Centre,
say, 50%
of budget

Tailor made
neighbourhood
provision,
say, 45%
spent by the
Neighbourhood budget   Neighbourhood
of say, £5m.   Partnership

This illustration shows us both how radical are the implications of the mild phrase 'bending budgets' and, thus, how difficult it will be to persuade Statutory Partners to go down this road to renewal. Yet, go down it they must. So, it is probably the case that Government will have to be prescriptive as well as being persuasive. However, prescription may merely cause resentment unless, at the same time, those who do the prescribing also spell out exactly why they are doing it and exactly what the benefits and objectives of the exercise are all about – harnessing the talents and energies of the resident customer in neighbourhoods to help to choose the service which they need and to prevent the need for some services. Once again, the teaching powers of the Residents Academy will be valuable, this time to show officers how to 'do' less and 'enable' more.

Other assets

So far, however, we have been considering how to budget for and provide public services differently. However, we also need to consider how to look after and use public property and physical assets differently. These questions arise:

- Can Voluntary Organisations and/or the Local Neighbourhood Forum look after and use the local Sports Centre, Baths and public open space differently?
- How can we best care for the many mini 'confused' public spaces which litter most urban neighbourhoods, the ownership of which have been lost in the mists of time. As in Balsall Heath, could they be best given to the resident who lives next to it or to the local neighbourhood Forum?
- Can housing, other public buildings and land which are currently lying idle be used in more enterprising ways to generate money and further increase income to drive additional local services or to build social capital? Recall, by looking after public housing differently in Balsall Heath some £75m was raised. In Castle Vale, tenants who manage their own housing stock invest £1.3m of their rental income of £12m in socially useful ventures.
- If a socially aware Richard Branson was responsible for a neighbourhood's assets, how would he use them to add social value to them?

Land and Property

Acquiring real wealth

Residents and their Partners will gain even more powerful teeth if they also acquire buildings and land which they can manage and from which they can realise an income with which to drive renewal forward.

The residents of Royds in Bradford were given land, residents in the Coin Street neighbourhood of London were given property and land. These enlightened transfers of property and assets gave real teeth to those who managed them. The same happened when HMG ensured that Colleges acquired their own land, schools gained their own budgets and Housing Action Trusts acquired their own houses!

If we are to expect neighbourhoods to emerge from decades of confused dependence and lack of responsibility to a new era of independence and responsible conduct then they need to be given and trusted to manage the public land and assets which fall within them.

Planning – is an asset if placed in local hands

At first glance, residents will feel that their Neighbourhood Development Plan should include social, educational, safety and other 'soft' issues. However, at second glance, residents will realise that if they possess hard assets – land and buildings – they will be able to fund and advance the soft side of their plan.

So, as each neighbourhood becomes excavated individually from beneath the collective culture of dependency of the Welfare State in which it had been entangled, it will not just gain assets but the ability to manage them well and productively. Thus, as part of its Development Plan, each neighbourhood will need an Asset Management Plan for realising the maximum use of them.

Even the most casual glance at urban development over recent decades shows that land and property development in neighbourhoods has paid scant regard to the developmental needs of these neighbourhoods and more to Citywide needs.

If each neighbourhood had their own plan this would not happen. It would then be easier for each neighbourhood to develop and maintain their own asset base and identity. For this reason, the Neighbourhood Manager needs to be joined not just by the neighbourhood's equivalent of a school bursar or budget holder, but by a person with significant entrepreneurial flair.

The Neighbourhood's Social Entrepreneur will need to be its own mini Richard Branson, its own Economic Entrepreneur. For, they will need to be able to ask – and answer – such questions as these:

- As with Castle Vale, can the Council's and Housing Association stock be transferred to a Neighbourhood Association which manages them is such a way which makes them both cared for and able to fund other neighbourhood functions?
- Can vacant land, invariably dumped on and litter strewn, have housing and some other development built on it to local social and financial advantage?
- Are there public buildings which are idle or underused and ill-managed, which can be run in more imaginative and enterprising ways?

Every depressed neighbourhood contains public assets which, if managed in entrepreneurial ways, could be used much more productively. If run as part of the vast bureaucracies of the Welfare State, these potentially rich assets are a confused and valueless part of a monopoly which nobody will use or buy. If, however, they are seen as part of a locally owned neighbourhood venture, they could realise significant funds, render external grant aid for renewal redundant and contribute to the sustainable renewal of the neighbourhood.

A Social/Economic Entrepreneur, perhaps seconded by Business in the Community from a thriving private sector company, could be worth their weight in gold to a struggling, apparently poor, but potentially rich neighbourhood. Just as in the case of Trades Unionism, the High Street can be of great value to the Back Street.

From Town Hall to Neighbourhood Hall

The renewal of so many Town and City Centres has been driven by the Town Hall/Council House and its Town Centre Manager in partnership with the private sector. Each urban area has been helped in this task because there has been a focal point for this renewal – the Civic Centre, the Town Hall and Council House.

It follows that each neighbourhood needs its own Civic equivalent of the Town Hall, a Neighbourhood Civic Centre where the team of Neighbourhood Strategic Partners and Neighbourhood Manager can be based. This neighbourhood centre could be a Church or Community Hall, a school, a Library or a Sports Centre. It will differ from neighbourhood to neighbourhood.

What would a modern Police station look like if designed for tomorrow's world? Or, a Health Centre? Or, a Library? Or, a base for a Neighbourhood Manager and Capacity Builder? Far from being separate buildings separately managed, would they be housed in one new (or old) building? Would they be a kind of One-Stop-Social-Shop in the way today's Tescos and Morrisons are one-stop commercial shops? Want to see an example of one of these? Go to Stoke. They call theirs a 'First-Stop-Centre'. Any self respecting village has a village hall. A renewing neighbourhood needs its Neighbourhood Hall in which its joined-up services, neighbourhood staff – and budget – can be found.

Thus, it is certain that if we are to inject into each neighbourhood the ownership, pride and purpose which a home owner or a Town Hall can generate, then the following are essential:

- A Neighbourhood Strategic Partnership.
- A Neighbourhood Manager.
- A Neighbourhood Budget.
- A development plan for using physical as well as social neighbourhood assets productively.
- A Neighbourhood Centre in which the team of neighbourhood partners are based, one of whom is an Economic Entrepreneur.

But, all this is far easier said than done. It's one thing to ask the passive resident to become the Active Citizen with the help of a Community Organiser. It's an even more difficult thing to ask the top-down 'doing' State to move from its Empire to becoming a neighbourhood enabler and to end up with both one overarching Town Hall/Council House and also as many Neighbourhood Halls as there are neighbourhoods. So, Government needs to set a clear and unequivocal lead and the Residents Academy needs to put the relevant courses in place for Officers and Councillors as well as residents.

Key Questions

The 'Communities and local Government' committee is an all party House of Commons committee charged with looking at the expenditure, administration and policy of Department for Communities and Local Government. In November 2011 it issued a report titled 'Regeneration'. It said: "Ministers have no adequate strategy to address the complex problems faced by England's most deprived communities. If further resources for regeneration are not found, there is a risk that major problems will be stored up ..." It went on to say that: "Across the country, regeneration projects have stalled or stopped completely as funding reductions and the absence of finance have taken their toll."

Yet, this chapter and the last one have explained how Balsall Heath, Castle Vale and a few other bottom-up neighbourhood initiatives show that devolving a Neighbourhood Budget and the local use of assets can easily provide all that is needed to solve those problems identified by this Committee. On the one hand, the Committee is right. Using existing money and assets in existing ways wastes money. Cuts merely reduce the amount of money being wasted. But, in place of cuts, we can now clearly see on the other hand how very large sums of money can be created by using existing money differently, via prevention and via the effective use of underused assets.

So, a major question becomes: Why are we not using this money and these assets in this way? Why are we wasting them? Why has the plea of the resident customer not been heard or acted upon? And, in future, what has to be done to make us stop wasting them and to start realising their huge potential? How can the lessons learned from the success of Balsall Heath and a few other neighbourhoods be widely replicated? What role can and should central Government play in this replication? Can it help the Empire of the Welfare State to move to the Commonwealth of the Welfare Society?

In late 2011, the Department for Communities and Local Government (DCLG) set up some 120 Neighbourhood Planning Pilots and 10 Budgeting Pilots to answer these questions and show how they can be applied in many neighbourhoods. Balsall Heath is one of both of these pilot initiatives. The next chapter shows how Government and DCLG could themselves be helped if they too changed to meet the needs of a transformed bottom-up and top-down.

Chapter 8

REINVENTING GOVERNMENT TO ENABLE THE RENEWAL OF NEIGHBOURHOODS

Every once in a while society turns a corner, leaves one stage of human development behind and evolves a new phase of existence. The Enlightenment's advocacy of scientific reason and application of it to our mastery of the material world was one such new phase. So also was the Welfare State as Government took responsibility for caring for all citizens and supplying them with the services, which we have discussed. But, this major step forward is now over 100 years old and, as our findings show, has run its course.

To put things right, politicians of the left would extend and develop the State as it exists. Some of those on the right would dismantle and diminish it. These views are respectively derived from ideologies of collectivism and individualism. But, the residents and organisers of Balsall Heath and other recovering neighbourhoods suggest a more practical solution. They don't want to diminish the national State and its local manifestations so much as to alter the way it works, to change its emphasis from doing things 'to' people over large tracts of administrative land to doing things 'with' people by 'enabling' them to do things for themselves. This entails a new compact between the State and its people in which both parties have to make a new partnership of equals work at neighbourhood level. In place of relating to each other once a year or every 5 years via a vote, the State and residents need to find ways of partnering each other every day of the year.

The new partnership is sensibly called a Welfare Society. While the Welfare Society will need to tax people it will use significant parts of those taxes differently by putting them in the entrepreneurial hands of the resident customer, not the monopolistic hands of the Civil Servant. As we have seen, the result is financially, as well as socially, very rewarding especially at a time of national austerity.

The old saying: "Why didn't I think of that sooner?" is relevant. For, decade after decade we have supplied expensive services to resident customers and initiated many costly renewal programmes to make good the deficiencies of the services – and still it did not deliver the goods.

It took a Community Organiser, a Trades Unionist and a corner shop keeper to work out a more cost effective alternative. Anne Power and Emmet Bergin documented a number of similar initiatives in their powerful book, Neighbourhood Management written in 1999. A key question becomes: "How do we go about replacing the Welfare State with this new way of caring for people via a Welfare Society?" For, won't those who theorise about, staff and preside over the old Welfare State resist? No Empire has ever easily changed to give power to its once dependent colonies. So, if we are to create a Commonwealth of Neighbourhoods we will need real leaders, a clear plan of action and prescriptive powers.

This chapter discusses how an imaginative central government can help to speed recovery from the bottom-up and help it to form a new productive partnership with enabling Councils and other Statutory Players. The chapter which follows this one will show how renewing the sense of moral authority will give a unifying point and purpose to that partnership.

Especially for Civil Servants, Government Ministers and Shadow Ministers

Prescription

In the past, Civil Servants and Government Ministers have relied too much on persuasion and not enough on prescription and have seen renewal as an add-on to existing practices and not as being part of a major practice.

This chapter shows both Civil Servants, Ministers and their shadows why active residents need them to be more direct and focussed if they are to become empowered to form productive partnerships with newly reformed Statutory Partners.

Unless Whitehall plays its part in this, renewal is unlikely to take place in very many neighbourhoods. Residents and local Statutory Professionals really do need the very active and clear sighted support of Whitehall if they are to make substantial progress. So far, the words have been good, but the deeds lag far behind.

The House of Commons Public Administration Select Committee reported recently (Summer 2011) its views on the way Government and Whitehall were fairing with the delivery of Neighbourhood Empowerment and the Big Society. They concluded that "We find that while the Government seeks to embrace change, they have failed to recognise the scale of the reform required or to set out the change programme required to achieve this reform .... (there is) antipathy to a plan for reform ... coordination from the centre and strong political leadership. As a result, key policies like the 'Big Society' agenda and decentralisation will fail." They recommend "a change programme (which) would enable real change in Whitehall and avoid the fate of previous unsuccessful reform initiatives..... Ministers seem to believe that change will just happen .... (It won't)." So, what is the solution? What might that 'change programme' look like?

First, we need to add 'prescription' to 'persuasion' if we are to succeed. But, we all know that Central Government fears being prescriptive to Local Government. It sees it as being the local representative of the people. In future, Central Government needs to see key parts of Local Government as an impediment to the empowerment of people in neighbourhoods.

If action and good outcomes can be achieved by consensus all is well. But, in the past, the consensual approach has not worked. At the end of the day, the people who have lost out are the many millions who live in the many thousands of excluded neighbourhoods. They can't be allowed to continue to suffer and feel excluded. They are the customer. They are the tax-payer. They are the ones in need of support.

Thus, as an end resort prescription can and should be used. It may even be that the very threat of it will concentrate the mind. But, as with the failing school or LEA which is closed, prescriptive action against a few Local Authorities may persuade the large majority to follow consensual guidance. If Government wants success it must grasp this nettle and practice 'tough love'.

Government must change

Before it can become bold and determined enough to grasp the nettle Government must itself change. For many decades the great departments of the State have been built up and resourced to help local government and other Statutory Partners to provide specialist services to people. And, when they failed, it has provided time-limited extra top-down grants on top of these services. It has not changed them. That is, the Government's attempts to renew neighbourhoods have been expensive and well-intentioned but disjointed and lodged in different, often contradictory, bits of different Departments of State. They have failed to connect in real partnerships with real people. There has been no department specifically designed to drive the renewal of civil society, the empowerment of people, the reform of services and budgets to aid that empowerment.

So, we propose to reinvent Government and help it to empower Active Citizens with the help of a new Department of Civil Renewal. It will join up Government thinking and action in both Whitehall and the Town Hall, drive it right down to neighbourhood level, give power to people, help to put them in charge of their own destiny and enable them to make a lasting difference to the quality of their lives in a new compact with the state.

Some people wanted to do this over 100 years ago. In the late 1800's the Mutual Societies, Co-operators and Trades Unionists could have gone on to invent a Welfare Society in which more and more people governed themselves, employed their own doctors, ran their own schools and created a Commonwealth of a Country. But, they didn't. They decided to go down the road which led to the Welfare State. During the 1900's this State came to deliver caring services 'for' and 'to' people, as in an Empire.

This worked for a while, even a long while. It fed the hungry, most of them, and housed the homeless, most of them. But, we now know that it has turned out to be a well intentioned but wrong choice. It made us dependent. Public housing now haunts us in graffiti strewn, high crime, no go areas. So, by the end of the 1900's, the Welfare State resulted in expensive, top-down, one-size-fits-all services which now fail to satisfy ordinary folk and reduce their ability to care for and help each other. We may be materially better off, but the quality of life and culture is poorer. We are in a social recession.

The answer to this problem entails creating in the first century of the new millennium a modern version of yesterday's mutualism in a just and renewed Civil Society. It entails a strong but enabling State, not fewer taxes but spending them in new ways which empower and inspire people to take control of their lives and agree their own agenda for the action which is needed to drive up the quality of life in the neighbourhoods where they live. The result will be a new compact between them and a modern State.

The great Departments of State were formed in a different industrial era of material need when it was possible to deliver uniform services to an uncritical and grateful population. In Beveridge's words, it was designed to respond to poverty, disease, ignorance, want and dependence. But, in tackling the former, it boosted the latter. Today, we face different social needs. We have a weak Civil Society and people require independence and Civil Renewal.

In the past, different bits of different specialist Government Departments which were based on want have tried to respond to this new situation. But, everyone knows they are not joined up, confuse people, are rarely managed by entrepreneurial risk takers and so have proved unable to drive the solutions needed from Whitehall through the Council House right down to neighbourhood and street level. By the time they arrive at street level they have been splintered, diverted and defeated by the holders of the mainstream budgets. They are very expensive, but also very ineffective.

So, we need to reinvent key parts of central Government. We need to:

1. Plan now to create a new Department of State which addresses the Social Recession, the need for Civil Renewal and the creation of Social Capital.

2. Take key parts from the Home Office, Communities and Local Government and one or two other bits from other departments and create a new, powerful and well resourced Department whose task is to Reinvent Government and facilitate Civil Renewal.

3. Insist that this Department will be second only to the Office of Prime Minister and the Treasury and give it these tasks:

    ▸ To knock together the heads of all other Departments to ensure a fully joined up Government agenda – not more initiatives, just one joined-up initiative to boost Civil Renewal.
    ▸ To drive forward on the Civil Renewal agenda with the help of a raft of entrepreneurial officials drawn from the voluntary and private sectors who are used to taking risks and acting in an entrepreneurial way.
    ▸ To get the State and Local Government off the back of ordinary people, putting them in control of their destiny and enabling them to enter into a new compact with a new State.
    ▸ To say the following to Local Government:

"We love you dearly and you are a vital feature of representative democracy. But, unreformed, you have become part of the problem. You are as relevant to today's voter as is the dock and mine of yesteryear. While they have moved forward and been replaced by flats, offices and high tech industry, you have not. Move with the times. Or even fewer people will vote for you. Become strategic, devolve all that you can right down to neighbourhood and street level – not all at once, or it will go pear shaped, but in a carefully managed series of rolling programmes of neighbourhood, civil and civic renewal which will take a generation to complete. Create a Neighbourhood equivalent (LMN) of LMS and ensure that those neighbourhoods whose residents are ready to handle it receive in year one 20%, year two 30%, and year three 50% of the budget which is spent in their area."

Say: "we won't tax you less. But, we will ensure that you will be able to use at least some of your taxes to better effect to create a just and good society. Help us to spend your taxes. We won't do it for you. We will do it with you. We will give you a Neighbourhood Budget created from existing mainstream expenditure, not from extra, time-limited funds."

In future, services which are tailor-made can only be delivered with the active participation of people. That participation can only be gained if it respects the diverse needs of the neighbourhoods where individuals live. Three things follow:

The boundaries via which many services are delivered must become coterminous with local neighbourhood boundaries, not remote administrative or existing political ones.

Services must become a joined-up part of an integrated neighbourhood agenda. It's not just Whitehall, but the Council House which needs to be re-invented to suit modern, diverse times.

Recipients must become responsible active participants and will require the help of a Community Organiser, Neighbourhood Manager and a Resident Academy to do so.

The following additional key functions for the new Department arise:

It needs to create an Ofsthood, an inspectorate of neighbourhoods. It's a disgrace that no failing neighbourhood has yet been 'formally failed', put into special measures and told: "You won't come out until you have improved in a, b and c ways. If, in a year, you have not improved, we will close down the existing management and give your budget to someone who (a) can manage it and (b) will hand it back to you when your capacity has been built."

The new department also needs to work with the Unions to help them to create a TUitC (Trades Unions in the Community). BitC (Business in the Community) has been a great success and has encouraged the High Street where customers shop to work with the Back Street where customers live. There should also be a TUitC enabling the Unions not just to help to improve the conditions of the worker in the work place but also in the environment where they live. Indeed, if Active Citizens are to be encouraged, they will need to apply the best work-based union organising principles to the places where they live. We really do need to foster a new sense of mutualism. Just as we need shop stewards to set industrial management on the right lines, so we need street stewards or street champions to act as modern good neighbours, the yeast of the neighbourhood.

If both Central and Local Government needs to be re-invented to respond to new social needs and the empowerment of residents, then it follows that the role of the elected representatives who manage Government must also change.

The role of the Councillor and MP in the Big Society

Since the voter first won the vote, the public sector has expanded. For the best of motives, it has come to do more and more for people. But, inadvertently, this has prevented people from caring for themselves and each other. It has turned the active resident and the thriving village in which they live into passive citizens and atomised places. So, we must now ask what the implications are of the transformation of Balsall Heath by Active Citizens for the role of the State and its representatives in future. How do we overcome these problems:

- For decades, fewer and fewer residents have voted for Councillors and MP's. For, they have not been able to see what they do, directly benefit from it or influence their actions.
- Once elected, Councillors and MP's have vanished from the voter's view into the Town Hall and Whitehall and only reappear, residents say, when they want your vote in 3 or 5 year's time.
- They have been dedicated to legislating for change to improve living conditions from the top-down via one-size-fits-all services which do good things 'to' people, not 'with' them.

Balsall Heath's transformation and the new role of the Community Organiser and the Neighbourhood Forum reverses that trend. Unable to get the services and quality of life they desire for themselves and their children from the politician and 'system', they have taken responsibility for transforming their own neighbourhood with dramatic results. Their involvement has made all the difference. Together, residents have achieved far more locally than any Councillor ever did. Residents have started to represent themselves in the neighbourhood where they live without regard to party. More, they have asked for their own neighbourhood budget so that they can shape the services they receive.

As a consequence, they have expected their recent Councillors to respond not just to their vote and to disappear into the remote Council House but also to respond to their everyday wishes. This implies a new, more productive, day-in-day-out relationship between the voter and their formal representative. Today, Balsall Heath's 3 Councillors have spent less time in the corridors of power and more in the streets and parks where their voters live. They bother with little every day issues and try directly to improve conditions at the level of the house, alleyway, street and park. This has little to do with party and a lot to do with care, concern and love. It heralds a new kind of representative and a non party approach to politics. The message from the neighbourhood to the politicians is this:

- Don't select candidates from the Party Faithful, but from amongst Active Residents.
- Don't expect Councillors and MP's to pursue Party Politics, but local issues defined by residents and, above all, their day to day needs.
- So, let Party Politics take a back seat and support the way residents organise themselves. The Big Society requires them to have a champion. These champions should be their Councillors and their MP in association with the Active Residents who staff the Neighbourhood Forum.

Becoming accustomed to this new role and practising it with skill will not be easy for the traditional Councillor or MP who has been used to horse-trading in the corridors and committee rooms of the Council House and Whitehall. So, in future those who select candidates to stand for Council will need to bare in mind the new people and the community skills required of them if they are elected. Our Residents Academy should come in very useful, both as a training ground for would-be Councillors and MP's and for inducting them into their new role once elected.

While the new role does not spell the end of political party choice, it certainly weakens it. For, the new skills required of the Councillor are less those of the party political activist versed in the theories and ideologies of their party and more those of the Community Organiser or Resident Activist. Indeed, the wise party machines would look less at their own kind to recruit a candidate and more to the up and coming ranks of Resident Activists.

Would this agenda and a new and more visible role for elected representatives be popular? Most people would vote for the Party which reinvented government, used taxes better, gave choice and control to the people, could envision an end to graffiti, litter, the fear of crime, create hope and opportunity, and reduce the credibility gap between the Politician and the people. Indeed, a measure of success would be if the vote doubled because people could trust and connect with the public sector.

Balsall Heath tells us that the time is ripe. The tipping point has been reached. Now is the moment to Reinvent Government and the role of the Councillor to enable Civil Renewal to take place, to strike a new bargain between the individual and the state.

The new Department of Government and the new kind of Politician required by the Active Citizen to help them to build a quality life in quality neighbourhoods must enmesh their work with the common sense of mutual responsibility and a regard for moral authority. We really can't just rely on good policies. We also need good people, we need to bring moral values to the centre of the social stage. The next chapter explains how these qualities can and should be developed with the help of our new Department of State.

Chapter 9

RENEWING MORAL AUTHORITY
AND THE SENSE OF RESPONSIBILITY

The best farmers have always known that if they don't steward the land well, put more back into it than they take out of it, then they can create a desert and starve.

The Stern report demonstrated convincingly that we have failed to apply this principle, burned too many fossil fuels, chopped down too many trees and flown too many planes. So, there is now a hole in the ozone layer which is causing global warming, the polar ice to melt, threatening the poor old Polar Bear as well as our coastal resorts and the Thames flood barrier.

But, the cure which Sir Nicholas Stern prescribed in not necessarily costly in financial terms. He recommended a change in our behaviour. He invited us to do such things as these:

- Take fewer flights.
- Drive less, walk more.
- Turn off the tap while brushing our teeth.
- A deterrent tax by Government on Airline Companies.
- Preserving trees.

Such remedies as these require a change of attitude and action, a change of culture. Will we take the advice?

We can't afford not to do so. But, an individual acting on their own will have little effect. It requires the whole neighbourhood and the whole nation, even the whole world to behave differently. That's a big ask. But, it's one to do with will and the sense of responsibility, not cash.

It is exactly the same with mending the fractured village and ending the social recession. We can only mend our fraught social life by behaving differently. The previous chapters show that this too does not cost more money. The key price which must be paid is, on the contrary, will and effort, in behaving with a greater sense of social responsibility. We cannot just rely on politics and government, important though they are. Morality, like charity, begins at home, locally. We don't just need good policies, we need good people, quality people, if we are to build good quality sustainable neighbourhoods. Please note that the words and argument of this and the next chapter follow very closely those which were first prepared for my previous book, Civil Renewal.

Rekindling moral authority – locally

What drives and motivates the Active Citizen? What binds them and their neighbours together in strong communities? What enables Active Citizens in strong communities to join in partnership with their Statutory Partners yet retain their independence? The answer has to be – shared subjective values and people with emotional maturity who command authority and who assert and uphold these values.

Beveridge Mark II

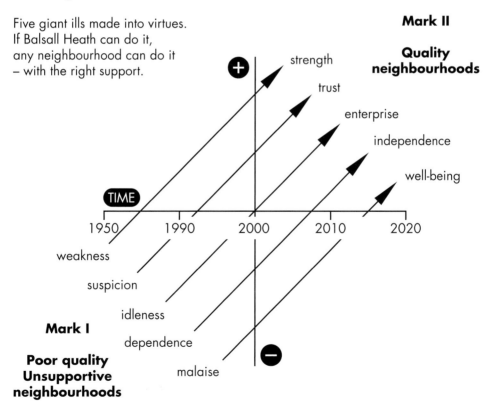

Five giant ills made into virtues.
If Balsall Heath can do it,
any neighbourhood can do it
– with the right support.

Mark II

Quality neighbourhoods

strength

trust

enterprise

independence

well-being

TIME

1950   1990   2000   2010   2020

weakness

suspicion

idleness

Mark I

dependence

**Poor quality
Unsupportive
neighbourhoods**

malaise

Yet, in today's world shared values and respect for authority are in short supply, particularly in the 3,000 excluded neighbourhoods which cause us most concern. As we discovered in earlier chapters about Balsall Heath, the Community Organiser and Active Citizens will be driven by mutual care and moral ends. But, they will need every bit of help they can get from national leaders and from our new Department of State if they are to turn these great ills – weakness suspicion, idleness, dependence and malaise – into these virtues – strength, trust, enterprise, independence and well-being in most neighbourhoods in the land. In effect, we need a Beveridge Mark 2 which can be pictured on the previous page.

Rekindling moral authority – nationally

If we expect these values and authority to be asserted from the bottom-up alone by Active Citizens and Community Organisers without help from national leaders from the top-down we will be waiting a long time for success. Even then, it will be sporadic and many areas will remain bleak. Universal success will depend on a concerted national effort which supports and encourages the efforts of leaders at the local level. Governments and politicians have not been used to trying to create values and morality. They must now get used to doing so – in close association with others via the proposed new Department.

Renewing the culture – The identity of place and the rites of passage

We need to be taught by our national leaders that:

- When the child is young and vulnerable its parent(s) and the wider local community should swear an oath of duty to care for, feed and look after them.
- This oath should include putting so much back into the environment of the place where the child grows up that he/she feels proud and safe in it.
- As each subsequent stage in the child's growth is passed, the child/adolescent/adult must return that care and mark it by also swearing an oath, so that in place of just receiving they also begin to give and recognise that by the end of their life they must have put back more into the community more than they have been given by it.
- Such things need to be taught in the home, in the community and in the school. Indeed, they should be taught in the way people live, not just in lessons in school but in the way the school and community are organised and the informal and formal codes by which social life is ordered and organised. They are, in effect, the 'standing orders' of life. They are the rites of passage.

Get the local culture right and the national culture will follow

Get the body language of the child-in-their-neighbourhood of origin right and we have the foundation upon which to build the common sense of citizenship. That is, having been cared for as a child, it becomes entirely reasonable that the adolescent should graduate from school by agreeing to invest their talents and ability to care for others back into their community.

Beyond that, upon reaching the age of 18, when the child is granted the adult right to vote, the new adult should inherit the responsibility to support the wider nation. Without this local-leading-on-to-national inheritance, the forces of law and order are powerless and James Bulger and Damilola Taylor will result again and again.

Every society known to mankind has had to create its own version of the above. The stages and rites of passage have always been marked by elders with ceremonies and customs, which have become woven into the tapestry and story of life.

In the case of our society, this tapestry of tradition has become faded and torn by the pace of change. It is no longer strong enough in the urban village for ordinary folk to hold onto. So, it is time that the elders or leaders of our nation – not just politicians, but people of faith, those in a position of communal leadership and parents – discuss how to weave a fresh tapestry appropriate to the changed circumstances of our modern age. Then, they need to impose it with authority and leadership.

Rights and responsibilities spelled out

Younger countries than ours, such as Canada, as well as older Eastern ones can teach us how to do this and contribute to our debate.

Our rites of passage, our induction and acceptance into adult maturity evolved and were passed on by custom and word of mouth in an unwritten constitution. Now that this glue has worn thin we have nothing in writing to fall back on which might tell us what to do.

Canada had no traditions and customs and so had to write things down and make some formal agreements to help its diverse people to stick together and respect each other. We should study its experience. Perhaps we should agree a few simple basic responsibilities which could be matched with rights and written in a freshly agreed list such as follows:

Rights given to the individual by Community & Country	Responsibility to Community and Country of the individual
Child Benefit	Caring for and teaching your own (& other) children to respect themselves, each other and the law of the land
Access to the NHS	Contributing to the health of the community, caring for its environment and being a good neighbour
Safety from crime	Reporting crime and serving on a jury
Social Security and other benefits	Paying taxes
Freedom of speech & information	Allegiance to Queen and country
The vote	Participating in communal affairs

A new year of Community Service

Once the list has been more elegantly and simply crafted, how might we present it to every young person in the land upon reaching, say, the age of 18?

Until relatively recently every young man had to do two years of National Service in the armed forces. Many benefited, especially youngsters from difficult backgrounds who instead of becoming involved in a violent gang, gained an education and had their character built. So, the nation also benefited.

In this day and age, young men and women would all benefit from a well organised robust year of Community Service which might be seen as a direct, if practical, part of their education, one specifically oriented to the arts, practices and values of citizenship.

Too many of us might still blink at the idea of making this year of communal service compulsory. So, perhaps it should at first be voluntary, but made more exciting by a number of incentives which might make it tomorrow's version of today's 'gap year'. It might count towards an NVQ, Degree and other certificates. Those undertaking it might get a 50% reduction on the repayment of their student loan.

Couldn't or rather shouldn't, the proposed new Department of Civil Renewal be charged with organising this year? It may, of course cost them a bob or two. But, the civil renewal benefits would render it cheap at the price.

On February 18th 2004, the Chancellor spoke to a conference of the National Council of Voluntary Organisations and suggested that 'a call to service among young people' might become the norm. Ruth Fox and Thieu Besslink (Connecting People, the Fabian Society, 2004) wrote that 'such a clarion call to service for young people across the UK would be a seminal moment in our history'.

Having learned about 'citizenship' in theory as part of the national curriculum in schools, by practical engagement in the community for a year after school 'young people would learn about the institutions of civic society and develop a sense of trust in each other and the organisations they serve'. A wide range of community service placements might be considered, such as these:

- A voluntary or community organisation.
- Teaching primary age children to read or mentoring a difficult pupil.
- Conservation and environmental works.
- Working in a hospital or with social services.
- Working with a faith group.
- Service overseas.

There is the prospect of a veritable army of young people who could, if well organized, accomplish a great range of socially valuable tasks which would not otherwise be undertaken – and, in the process, become better citizens able to steward social life as more aware and concerned adults.

The Graduation Ceremony

Passage from the practical School of Community Service warrants a Graduation Ceremony and the presentation of a Certificate which enshrines the Citizen's Rights and Responsibilities and surrounds and celebrates it with a fair bit of pomp and circumstance.

Newcomers from elsewhere now have to undergo an induction ceremony into the citizenship of this country. That's fine. But, shouldn't every person, including all those born here as well as newcomers, have to undergo a 'rite of passage' signifying their inclusion into adult citizenship? Shouldn't everyone have to go through this special graduation ceremony, accept the rights and, in return, swear to undertake the concomitant responsibilities, which the year is intended to instil and explain?

The ceremony might take the form of a school prize giving ceremony combined with the atmosphere of a community carnival or celebratory meal. The Queen Mother's funeral and the Golden Jubilee celebrations remind us all that we can be quite good at enjoying ourselves and engaging in a bit of Midsummer Night revelry. The ceremony should be full of fun as well as gravity.

So, the celebration of each and every person's Graduation into Adult Citizenship should become the most noteworthy of the rights of passage, a cause not just of a communal celebration within a neighbourhood but of a national one.

Some 60 years ago, the 11th hour of the 11th day of the 11th month became Remembrance Day. Everyone now stops for a moment at that time each year and Whitehall and the Cenotaph host a special event to honour those who gave their lives so that others might live.

As our unwritten constitution evolves and we slow the pace of change to capture the concept of our mutual interdependence and emphasise the duty of the young to their community and country, couldn't we have an annual Day of Duty when all in that year who Graduate into Adult Citizenship are honoured, perhaps at a ceremony of Youthful Maturity to be led by a 'Prince of all the Faiths,' but not a politician.

With the help of schools, faith leaders and community organisers, this could put pride into people, their neighbourhood, their city and their country. Whilst Politicians could encourage debate aimed at such an outcome, they couldn't possibly lead it unless they were not just agreed but enthusiastically united in a cause which was above and beyond party political interest. They would need the keen support of all key players – faith, school and community leaders.

They would need to see that this was at once intended as a lasting epitaph to Damilola Taylor, James Bulger, Stephen Lawrence, Holly Wells and Jessica Chapman and an acknowledgement by us all that if the Queen can: 'Vow to Thee my Country', then so can each and everyone of us, in a Day of Duty and a Celebration of Commitment to others which binds us all together in Civil Society.

Jonathan Sacks, the Chief Rabbi, reminds us that the key word in biblical ethics is 'covenant'. In a covenant, "parties come together to pledge themselves to a code of mutual loyalty and protection. Unlike a contract, a covenant is born in the recognition that no individual can achieve his or her ends in isolation. Because we are different, we each have strengths that others need, and weaknesses that others can remedy. Unlike a contract, however, a covenant is more than a narrow legal agreement bound by mutual interest. It involves a commitment to go beyond the letter of the law, and to sustain the relationship even at times when it seems to go against one's personal interest.

A covenant is an agreement in which higher moral force, traditionally God, is either a direct party to or guarantor of a particular relationship. The idea of covenant reminds us that there are some rules whose claim upon us are stronger than short-term self-interest and involves a commitment to the institutions into which we were born and from which our identify derives."

A movement to renew the social environment

In place of strife and political discord, something of a non and all-party and all-faith movement is emerging. After arising as a fringe concern, followed by a long period of both national and local discussion, most people now accept that the physical environment of the earth cannot indefinitely absorb the post enlightenment outputs of unrestrained scientific and industrial progress – excavations, emissions, pollution and toxic wastes – without serious damage being done to the land, sea and air. The environmentalists have shown us over the last 30 years that without links being made between personal responsibility and the common good the planet will be destroyed. Therefore, we are all beginning to apply the principles of stewardship to the natural environment so as to conserve it for the benefit of future generations. We all now worry about and seek to repair the hole in the ozone layer.

The same principles are now being applied to the social terrain. It is becoming increasingly clear that the foundations and guiding axioms of social and cultural life also do not have an infinite capacity to withstand the erosion which results from 'taking out more than is put in back in'. As with the earth, social life in developed countries like modern Britain has also been ravaged to such an extent by the age of industry, its organisational structures and concepts, that it has become impossible to maintain a civilised life in key parts of the nation. We really are in the middle of a social recession. So, the task of each succeeding generation must now be to steward society and leave the quality of social and cultural life, as well as the natural environment, in a better condition than when they found it.

In times past, change was so slow that the torn fabric of the community would be refurbished without many people having to think or act overtly about it. It just happened with the helping hand of grand-parent, doctor, priest and squire. Today, it will not. As a whole nation we all now need to consciously invest time and resources to discover and apply the best means of replenishing and sustaining community at the levels of family and local neighbourhood as well as in the wider society.

As with environmental stewards, the work of Community Organisers, Civic Entrepreneurs and Streets Stewards was at first isolated and unrecognised. They swam against the tide. They did not figure on the agenda of Politicians. Now, a sea change is taking place.

Changing the culture – Who can do what?

To find the will to create and sustain Civil Renewal and create a new Welfare Society in place of a Welfare State the new Department of Civil Renewal, which we propose, must ensure that all concerned are challenged and coordinated to play their full part, in ways such as these:

The State, central and local can:

Recognise the general problem and that the State itself became part of the problem because it came to do too much and has intruded too far into the communal sector, weakened its resolve and made it dependent.

Thus, like the Empire it needs to withdraw from the neighbourhoods of the communal sector in a phased way while enabling and funding them so that they can do more. It needs to fund Community Organisers and Neighbourhood Managers and the local associations they create.

This will entail switching its renewal programmes into being people led and not property and project led. It needs to turn them into Rolling Programmes of recovery in which the strong help the weak.

In particular, this means not just bending mainstream budgets, but finding very different ways of managing them so that people in communities have the resources and assets needed to deliver many of the services once provided for them by the State.

The new department of Civil Renewal should scrutinise every Central and Local Government policy and ask: Does it help to create a cohesive, stronger community/neighbourhood or not? How can this and other policies be made to have a more positive effect?

A more strategic, less doing, State and a more authoritative and resilient community entails the need for a new compact or partnership between Citizen and State.

Political Parties can:

- Contend with each other not to search for each other's weak spot and create conflict, but to play to each other's strengths and build a more consensual and enabling approach to what needs to be done.
- In place of their own party activists they can encourage active citizens to stand for Council seats.

Schools, Colleges and Universities can:

- Play an important role in developing children and families and their parents views of citizenship and the way we must care for and respect each other.
- Ensure the new year of civic duty in well organised, attractive to most and a highly valued component of each person's CV.
- Teach us all to understand and respect the Cathedral of Civilisation whilst also showing us how we can add to and develop it.
- Help us to respect science and pure reason, but place them within the wider context of the subjective value and quality of life.
- Support the Residents Academy.

The faiths can:

- Look beyond their immediate followers and set an example in the neighbourhoods where they are based.
- Revisit 'Faith in the City' and update it in an inter-faith exercise.
- Train priests in the skills and techniques of renewal and social entrepreneurship and make appointments with care.
- Talk to each other more and play an increased and mutually supporting role within the neighbourhoods in which they are based and in their governance.
- Demonstrate to us that the traditions and values of the newcomer from the East has much to teach the West and that, far from being a problem, they are part of the solution for which the whole nation yearns.

The voluntary sector can:

- Redouble its effort and recognise that it has a leading role to play in renewing social life.
- Prepare to take on the challenge of delivering more services from within the community.
- Support an army of Community Organisers, assist with their training and ensure they are supplied with the resources they need.
- Connect with and lead the Rolling Programmes of Neighbourhood Renewal.
- Demonstrate that Representative Democracy can only thrive if it is counterbalanced by strong Participatory Democracy.
- Work as one with Faith Establishments.

The private sector:

- Business in the Community, has a large role to play in putting back the things which it has taken out of communities and in showing both state and community how to be more enterprising.

- So too has TUitC, Trades Unionism in the Community. Today, we need to help people to organise in the places where they live, not just in the places where they work. The principles of organisation used by Trades Unionists in the places where people work should be applied to the creation of decent conditions in the places where they live and to raising the quality of life in excluded neighbourhoods.

Together the State, faiths, voluntary and private sectors can:

- Initiate and sustain not just action, but a series of regional debates about the need to mend our fractured social life and create sustainable Civil Renewal. These should feed into a National Debate or Conversation about the needs of civil society and the way we must care for each other. Whilst the State could play a significant part in facilitating this debate, it should be led by leaders of all the faiths, BitC, TUitC and the voluntary sector.
- The conversation should be sustained over a lengthy period and aim to reach a Tipping Point where the cultural tide turns, attitudes change and a new balance or covenant is reached between the community and other sectors of society.

Are our politicians and the new department we call for able to set the necessary moral lead? To make sure that they are, we need to revisit the party political ideologies which drive them and shape their view of society and how to improve it. Perhaps these ideologies need to change with the times. The next chapter explores the change required.

Chapter 10

POLITICS, CULTURE AND RENEWAL

Encouraging Active Citizens by Capacity Building, creating voluntary organisations, managing and funding neighbourhoods differently, asserting common values and leadership and reinventing Government have clear implications not just for a new relationship between participatory and representative democracy and the role of elected members but also for the ideologies of the political parties.

Ted, Raja, Naseem and Abdullah need their Councillors and MP to be unencumbered by the ideologies of the past which lead them away from the neighbourhood into the corridors of party political power. Instead, they require them to be able to focus clear sightedly on practical local matters for 365 days a year.

All the key ingredients needed to renew Civil Society and end the social recession in the many excluded neighbourhoods of the land have now been outlined and their interdependent nature discussed – with one exception. The culture of politics, the way Politicians envisage society and how they feel that it can be changed is the one major factor yet to be considered. Facing this factor will require real statesmanship from Politicians, their parties, advisors and an ability to stand back from their short-term party political interest and take a detached, long term view which is in the broader interests of society as a whole.

For a very long time, a major fault line has run through our politicians' culture and, thus, the way those who lead and staff the political and public services think. It is long standing, deep rooted and makes it difficult for them to see clearly the need for the radical reform of the services which they have grown accustomed to delivering. Hitherto, it has been possible to avoid recognising this and to argue that: "Services only don't work well because they don't have enough money. If only we can redistribute more wealth, they will improve." Yet, 40 years of costly renewal initiatives have not touched the problem. The excuse wears thin. Plus, the current period of austerity means that there is no more money. We must use existing money differently.

However, it is difficult to persuade those who are caught up in delivery to see that they are part of the problem when, for 150 years, they have thought that they were part of the solution. It is only human of them to find it difficult to agree that they are mistaken and that the foundation upon which they stand is built on sand, that the route they have taken is one of society's cul-de-sacs.

Since the days of Karl Marx in the mid eighteen hundreds, socialists have tried to extend the notion of collective self help from the working class work place and mutual society to the State in both economic and social affairs. One hundred and fifty years later, we now know that this theoretically derived attempt to manage the economy and run industry by collective planning simply did not work in practice. The individual entrepreneur who is responsible to his/her shareholders and the rigours of the market place have proved to be a far more enduring and effective way of producing and delivering a range of goods from which the customers can chose than the one-size-fits-all variety delivered by the collective state bureaucrat.

We tried very hard and for a long time to make the latter work in both Eastern Europe and the West. But, it simply did not deliver the goods. Thus, it has fallen by the wayside except in the practice and minds of a few who still yearn for the success of public collective production and mistrust, even despise, the private sector entrepreneur and their independent creation of economic capital.

Little wonder, therefore, that they find it almost impossibly difficult to apply the lessons of failure in economic life to a similar failure in social life. For, they can't see that the way we have 'nationalised' the way we care for each other and delivered one-size-fits-all social services in education, housing, environment, leisure and safety have also failed to work. Indeed, it has failed very badly indeed, particularly for all those who live in the 3,000 excluded neighbourhoods of the nation.

This failure of collective state socialism gave some Conservative thinkers hope. Having 'defeated' collective thinking in the economic sphere, they began to wonder if they could also do so in the social arena and, thus, privatise the caring services.

Yet, the social market follows quite different axioms from the private market. Unlike the customer who seeks to buy a new TV or fridge, the resident who wants a good park, school, environment and the sense of safety can't shop around and choose between different products. Merely, they want a better product, a more effective way of delivering it and a say over the quality and maintenance of it. They don't want a choice between different kinds of fish, just the right to make their own rod and to fish with it in their own pond.

This does not mean that all residents in all neighbourhoods have to provide everything for themselves. Far from it. But it does mean that the collective State itself should not always provide everything for them.

So, it's not the case that we need alternative parks or schools or environments from which we can choose, but alternative ways of managing the one local school, park and environment that we have in each neighbourhood. If such facilities are not to be managed centrally by the collective local authority, who can do it? There are a variety of alternatives to choose from which have been discussed in earlier chapters. They include:

- Residents might do it for themselves.
- The Neighbourhood Manager and their neighbourhood team.
- Once the local school has mastered the intricacies of its own management, is there any reason why it should not also look after the adjacent park or leisure centre if it wants to?
- Or, it could be the local housing association, Housing Action Trust or Tenants Organisation which might wish to also look after the environment, service the neighbourhood team or act as its accountable body.

It might even be the case that the local association of traders says: "Our High Street will thrive if the back street also thrives. So, we'll volunteer to market the new image of the neighbourhood and help the local school and housing association to advertise and fill its vacant posts. Further, just as most town centres now have a centre manager, our neighbourhood also need a manager. We'll provide and fund one." Thus, there is no need at all for the Neighbourhood Manager to emerge every time and everywhere from the public sector. They might be recruited either from the private or the voluntary one. There is no harm at all in injecting the attitudes and experiences of the private sector into the reformed public one. Indeed, BitC is currently en route to supporting the secondment of 1,000 private sector managers to work in neighbourhoods alongside the Community Organiser and Neighbourhood Manager.

Will all social services in all neighbourhoods be managed by one or other of the above in a set way? There is no one-size-fits-all alternative. Different combinations of the above will arise in different neighbourhoods. So, in some neighbourhoods, most if not all services may be delivered by devolved parts of the public sector via the neighbourhood management team. In others, a successful school might undertake the duty of maintaining the local park and swimming pool. In others, a Housing Association might do so. In yet others, a strong neighbourhood Forum or Voluntary Organisation might assume a leading role and maintain most local services. It's a case of horses for courses. In any one neighbourhood the key question for residents and politicians to ask is: "Which agency is best placed to deliver which service?"

That's the point of localism and self-determination. People in different neighbourhoods will make different choices. Diversity is inevitable. It works in those neighbourhoods which have tried it. We know that uniformity does not work in the many neighbourhoods which have suffered under it for several generations. So, let's go with what works and jettison a 150-year-old theory, which does not work.

Before some centralising collectivist cries that this is privatisation, it is necessary to remind them that it is the very opposite of privatisation. When we privatised an industry we took it out of collective State control and gave it to a private sector business to manage and run at a financial profit. The customer then either enabled it to succeed because they bought the product or they closed it down because they chose to shop elsewhere.

The proposed localisation of services places the management of them in the hands of groups of ordinary local people whose task is to help each other to improve the delivery of the product. This is mutualism, neighbourly self-help. It takes us back to the eighteen hundreds before we reneged on the principle of subsidiary and turned down the cul-de-sac which led from local self-help to remote central control.

Further, the neighbourhood plan which sets targets for the improvement of each service is worked out, implemented and reviewed by a combination of the Residents' Forum and the locally accountable Neighbourhood Team. That is, mutualism is far more locally accountable and flexible than central planning. And, it is very different indeed from privatisation.

There are three major prizes to be won by changing radically and localising the way many services are delivered. The first is that the quality of these services and life for millions of people will improve dramatically in the neighbourhoods where they live.

The second is that the political process will gain credibility because ordinary people will be able to (a) see that it can make a difference to their lives and (b) that they can influence it and be part of it. It is working for them and not for its own ideology. As the yawning credibility gap shrinks and is bridged it is, therefore, likely that the number of people who vote in local and national elections will increase. Indeed, increasing the number of people who vote from 20% to 50% in local elections should become a target and test of successful renewal.

The third is that we thereby necessarily change the 150 year old way we think about how to care for each other from being impersonal and remote to being personal and close at hand. Thus, we will change the way we act. It will make us behave better towards each other, to wish to give as well as to receive. It will make not just better policies, it will also make us better people. It takes us from the Welfare State to the Welfare Society. It helps us to end the social recession.

Collectivism and Individualism

A false distinction has been drawn in the past between the collectivism of socialism and the individualism of Conservatism. It is important to stress that while these concepts have been taken up over the last hundred plus years by different philosophers and political parties, as if one was right and the other wrong, they are in fact the inseparable, mutually dependent, flip sides of the same social coin.

The Cathedral of civilization is the cumulative collective work of many individual people toiling over many generations. The north wing is not independent. It can't stand on its own. It is not complete until the arched roof connects it to both the West Wing and the East one.

Yet, collectivism became separated by philosophers into one distinct way of seeing the world which was set against the allegedly opposed confines of choice and individualism. It is important to recognize that in the practical reality of life, they are not separate but integral, interconnecting, parts of a wider, more exciting, ebb and flow of the whole.

The development of an approach which combines the virtues of both collectivist and individualistic ways of organising social affairs could mark the end of a period of major debate and conflict between those who argued for a caring public state and those who have advocated private initiative.

As post-industrial society emerges from the cocoon of constraint, we must accept that it has for too long been supposed that only the well-educated 20 per cent of the population, the confident, ambitious and affluent are competent to run their own independent institutions, look after their own houses, use private health care and private schools and run their own businesses. Similarly, for too long it has been assumed that the poorly educated 80 per cent of the population were so incompetent and dependent that they could only be housed, made healthy and educated within one-size-fits-all institutions, which the State provided for them and that they not only could do none of these things for themselves but also that to dream of doing so should be positively discouraged.

It is no longer necessary to use such dated supposition and theories drawn from the past to form a policy which holds back the independent few in a vain, socially unbalancing, attempt to make them equal to the dependent majority and to uphold this act as if it were a caring virtue. Rather, the time has come when the natural privileges of independence and autonomy, which the ambitious were bold enough to forge for themselves, should be ungrudgingly offered to the many through the radical redefinition of the aims and functions of the State and the role of local Government.

Sir Ralf Dahrendorf made the point well when he said that in future 'individuals will have to appreciate that philanthropy is a social obligation; companies will have to understand that it is in their enlightened self-interest' to give and to be involved in the life of the community in which they are situated. Above all, said Sir Ralf, 'we need a pact between Government and the voluntary sector which preserves all the sensitivity and flexibility of private action, but involves a major share of Government funding.' The neighbourhood's use of its own budget and the entrepreneurial functions of the Community Organisers and Civic Entrepreneur illustrate that 'Government funding' does not mean 'grant' aid or the 'redistribution' of wealth but the use of finance and the organisation of society in quite different and new ways.

So, the third way is not a compromise between the extremes of left and right collectivism and individualism. It aims to blend the best of these worlds together. In so doing, it aims to include the third force of active citizens in the management of their own lives in the neighbourhoods where they live and raise their families.

Once participatory democracy and the governance by people of their own neighbourhoods becomes the order of the day, then conventional party politics becomes largely redundant, especially at the local level. Most people are not concerned with political theory but with more practical matters. Is there litter in my street and, if so, how do I get it moved? Are my child and my neighbour frightened to go out at night and, if so, how can I help them to feel safer? And so on. These are practical, every day, all party and non-party questions, which require answers that are not prejudiced or predicted by theory or political caucuses.

It is increasingly difficult to grasp that anyone can ever have supposed that the route to social progress was via party political conflict and victory or loss by one or another 'side' in work between workers and management and in politics between the poor and the rich, the haves and have-nots. But, they did and influential politicians still do. Lord Hattersley was still insisting, even in 1998, that "the call for consensus is wrong" and that to determine issues "on their merit" is "dangerous for socialism". Yet, it is clear to most people that we must play to each other's strengths, not attack each other's weaknesses or accentuate our capacity to distrust and beat each other. Bringing the different sections of a community and the wider society into mutually productive alignment is not a "compromise" but an energizing and liberating virtue. Indeed, bringing different interest groups together does more than create a simple sum of them. It gives added value. It creates communal bonds and mutual understanding which ties people together and generates fresh energy, growth, 'flair' and 'flow'. In helping others rather than vying with them, we help ourselves and multiply rather than redistribute scarce resources.

It follows that just as the bankrupt mill and mine of the industrial era must close and be superseded, so also the failing services and party political culture of the industrially derived Welfare State must be closed down and reopened under new management to suit a new purpose.

Too often in the past Politicians have supposed that they know best and that ordinary people, especially those in the most difficult areas in the country, can't play any part in their own solution. We now know that this no longer holds true, if it ever did.

Ordinary people know rather more than Politicians about what is right for them and their neighbourhoods. With the careful encouragement which a new breed of Community Organiser and Civic Entrepreneur can give, local people and local businesses hold many of the answers to questions which have bedevilled us for 100 years. It is now clear that the role of local and central Government is not to impose solutions but to devise policies which enable more local solutions. It needs to stop giving people fish and to start teaching them how to fish for themselves.

Many of the assumptions and political dichotomies of the twentieth century seem destined to fade as a fresh and radical alternative emerges, a third way which entails using neither the public nor the private sectors alone to deliver services. The woefully weakened "third" or "community" sector can, if strengthened, play a vital role – which also changes the black and white way we view the public and private sectors. The community sector can rejuvenate Civil Society close to home, where most people find their identity, well-being and purpose in life.

These developments are progress not privatisation, liberation not competition. They change the very nature of Government and entail a new compact or covenant between the people and local and central Government. In addition to good people in neighbourhoods we need good, caring, people in the Town Hall and in Whitehall, ones who are driven more by faith than by redundant party politics.

This covenant is about to be invited onto the centre of the stage by a range of voices calling from the four corners of the land. They can be heard in Bromley by Bow, Birkenhead, Toxteth, Easterhouse, Castle Vale and Balsall Heath. For some time these voices were hesitant and spoke in whispers. Then, they became an audible buzz. Today, the sound they make has risen to become a clarion call to unite the nation and propel us through the first decades of the new Millennium.

Tomorrow, they will be joined by the cries of success which flow from the newly formed Neighbourhood Planning and Budgeting Pilots.

Will the most senior Politicians, clerics and opinion leaders hear these cries? Will they respond to them with a more adequate understanding of how society works? Will they, therefore, roll up their sleeves, become the champions of people in neighbourhoods and enable the bottom-up to work in productive and practical harmony with them? Well, to give them credit, they did set up these pilots. They did ask them to report on progress and how to replicate success in many neighbourhoods. That's got to be good news and real progress.

Chapter 11

THE WAY FORWARD –
A PROGRAMME OF ACTION

It is important to repeat the fact that no Empire ever gave up its dependent Colonies voluntarily and without a struggle, even when the practical common sense of it stared it in the face. Its fingers had to be prized off its possessions with a degree of force. We must expect the Welfare State to do the same. Indeed, making that expectation overt is the first step to be taken in moving forward towards the new Welfare Society. For, it tells us that we must use a degree of prescription and not just rely on persuasion which can and has been ignored.

Balsall Heath may have made remarkable progress. But, it has been a 30 year long painful uphill process. Even though the neighbourhood's local Partners have become sympathetic and done much good work, the Police and others still don't know what their budget is. So, even in Balsall Heath there is still some distance to travel before all the potential of the new Welfare State can be realised and the process of renewal is sustained and quickened.

If this is the experience of Balsall Heath, it is little wonder that the message to residents in many onlooking neighbourhoods has been: "Why bother? You'll only get hurt. It's too hard. Don't try. If Balsall Heath finds it so difficult what hope have we got?" So, what is to be done? How can Government and other neighbourhoods be helped to speed the process and replicate Balsall Heath's successes?

On the one hand, as with colonies struggling to become independent of the Empire, residents must simply get on with the job of transforming their neighbourhood and putting as much pressure as possible on their statutory colleagues to invest in their work and devolve staff and budgets to neighbourhood level.

On the other hand, if we leave change to previously passive residents then it will be fitful and slow. So, we must insist that the Empire reforms itself and accepts that 'if it goes with the flow' and acts on the messages it gets from its pilots then it will create an exciting new enabling and cheaper role for itself. It will become a hugely important new Commonwealth. That is, we must ask all those sympathetic Ministers and their opposition counterparts to rise to the occasion, demonstrate real and forceful leadership and show both Whitehall Departments, local Government and Statutory Players just what is expected of them in the new world of Active Citizens and the Big Society. If they are to do this, then they will need to take the following steps:

1. Change the culture

- We need leaders from all the faiths and all the parties to come together and lead a national and regional culture changing debate, which guides each of us into behaving differently, mending the hole in the tattered social ozone layer and ending the social recession.
- We need to re-moralise society and show that social life will only flourish if all people come to play an active and responsible role in building and sustaining it. The citizen must cease to be passive and begin to play a major part in the sustenance of the village in which they live. We need to stop giving people fish and enable them to fish for themselves.
- We need Government to agree a number of practical developments to flow from this culture and attitude changing debate. These should include a form of National Social Service in which all teenagers should participate.
- We need to tie this Social Service to a Rite of Passage in which each community welcomes its older teenagers into adult life and require of them a range of social duties.
- We need these leaders to persist month after month, year after year until the culture is changed and we can see a Welfare Society taking the place of the Welfare State.

2. Multiplying Community Organisers and Neighbourhood Managers

- We need to encourage at least one Community Organiser in every neighbourhood to step forward and act like a community equivalent of a shop steward. We need to enable that organiser to be employed by fellow residents and help them to form a Forum which both represents their neighbourhood and helps it to become strong and robust.
- Locality is already en route to helping to do this. It needs every help and encouragement. In particular, it needs at least one Statutory Partner or a

number of them in each neighbourhood to invest in that post to permanently sustain it and to place alongside it a Neighbourhood Manager. That Manager needs to be tasked with co-ordinating a neighbourhood team, a neighbourhood plan and a devolved neighbourhood budget.

3. Change the Government and Whitehall

- We need the Government to take up and implement the suggestions of its Public Administration Scrutiny Committee.
- It needs to set up a new tailor-made Big Society Civil Renewal Department which is specifically geared to helping all other Departments, Local Government and Statutory Players to focus on creating social capital and enabling ordinary residents to build the village we all need to house, feed and love us.
- This Department needs to be staffed by experienced practitioners, not the usual Civil Servants who have no coal face experience or enthusiasm.
- And, it needs to be led not just by Politicians from the Government, but from all the parties. For, this is a society-wide issue, not a party political or ideological one.

4. Change the way local Government and other statutory players are structured

- Supporting Neighbourhood Management, Neighbourhood Strategic Partnerships and neighbourhood budgeting and investing to save is not an optional extra. It is a must.
- The changes must not be funded centrally but from existing mainstream budgets using the logic of 'investing to save'.
- And, we need to find Councillors (and MP's) who will act less as Party Activists and more as Community Champions and work hard to reform 'the system' in favour of devolution and empowerment.
- Councils and Government need to praise succeeding Pilot and Guide Neighbourhoods and support them in spreading the message laterally, not in top-down ways, via the proposed Rolling Programmes of Renewal.

5. Set up a Residents' or Neighbourhood Academy in each Urban area

- Each Urban area needs its own Residents Academy.
- Each Academy will need to be staffed part-time by a number of experienced practitioners supported by a branch of the local University so that certificates can be given. Equip it to train, mentor and multiply these people:

- ▸ Community Organisers
- ▸ Active Citizens
- ▸ Neighbourhood Managers
- ▸ Officers from all statutory agencies
- ▸ Councillors and MP's

6. Support Guide Neighbourhoods and Rolling Programmes of Neighbourhood recovery

- The recovery we call for is not easy. It will take a generation to achieve. So, it is unlikely that it can be achieved everywhere all at once. With the coordinating help of our new Government Department. Community Organisers, Neighbourhood Managers, Local Councillors and other Statutory Players are advised to create a series of Rolling Programmes of Recovery in each urban area. Start with one, then 5, then more neighbourhoods over a period of 10 years. Get it right in the first neighbourhood, then in the next 5. Call these Guides, then challenge them to help and include the next set of neighbourhoods until all are included. Government needs to insist that these programmes develop swiftly and in cases where this does not happen, it needs to intervene as if they were a failing school.

- Not only will this help residents in neighbourhoods to proceed at a manageable pace, it will also help the Government, Council and other statutory players to ease the strain as they move from Empire to Commonwealth.

- It will also help if we point out that each neighbourhood will gradually go through a number of steps en route to recovery. The first step on the rung should be the Community Organiser. Next might come the Neighbourhood Manager who will, with the organiser, set up an NSP, Neighbourhood Plan, Neighbourhood Budget and so on. Different neighbourhoods might pause at one or other rung. Some might well halt before they reach the top horses for courses. So, each authority area may well end up with a range of ladders, one for each neighbourhood, where the players are at several different levels. Those who have progressed furthest will, no doubt with the help of the Residents Academy, entice others to take the next steps.

The ladder of renewal steps

Just as we will end up with a range of ladders in one authority area, so also we will end up with a range of ladders in each different authority area as we all combine to change the way we structure our support for each other.

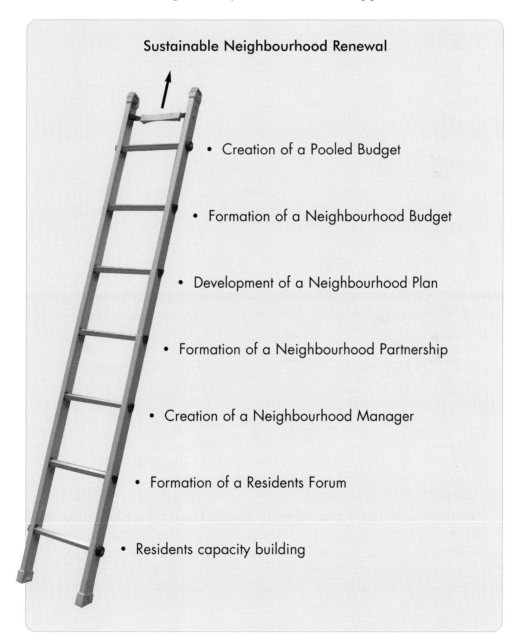

Sustainable Neighbourhood Renewal

- Creation of a Pooled Budget
- Formation of a Neighbourhood Budget
- Development of a Neighbourhood Plan
- Formation of a Neighbourhood Partnership
- Creation of a Neighbourhood Manager
- Formation of a Residents Forum
- Residents capacity building

7. Moral Authority

- The new Department of Civil Renewal must tackle the major sins facing society in the new millennium – idleness, weakness, suspicion, dependence and malaise. It will need to harness the energies of all the major faiths and to help Politicians to develop their vocabulary to include morality and ultimate values. For, without these there will be no glue with which to bind together each neighbourhood village and motivate Active Citizens to reach further and further up their ladder of renewal.

8. The end of ideology and the need for a new kind of politics and Politician

- Many of the attitudes enshrined in the political parties are 100 years old and relate respectively to collectivism and individualism. Re-building life in atomised neighbourhoods and re-creating the way the State cares for people requires us to see these different perspectives as being flip sides of the same social coin. That is, we need to begin to create a new kind of political way of thinking which relates to the very practical needs of citizens and not those of the political parties. In turn, we need to find a new generation of political representative whose formative influences rely less on the Party Politics of left and right and more on their efforts to champion the renewal of their neighbourhood.

9. Leadership

- The all party leadership of the new Government Department of Civil Renewal will wish to set targets for and actively encourage improvements in the quality of life in neighbourhoods and receive regular progress reports from each urban area. It will also need to set up an Ofsthood capable of identifying success and failure and, where necessary, putting a neighbourhood or whole authority area into special measures. For, success will depend on conveying conviction and real determination.

The outstanding question is this: Do we really have the determination to succeed? A real measure of that determination is whether we are prepared to dismantle many of the institutional caring structures and budgets of the top-down Welfare State and construct in their place those of a new Welfare Society in which the individual in the neighbourhood where they live has a new and pivotal role to play.

If we falter in our resolve we should reflect on 4 things:

1. The vast amounts of tax-payer's money spent on renewal initiative after initiative over the last 40 years only resulted in there being more excluded neighbourhoods, not less.
2. James Bulger, Stephen Lawrence, the riots of midsummer 2011 and all the many residents who live such sad and unfulfilled lives.
3. The fact that Balsall Heath, significant other neighbourhoods and the new Pilots show that there is a different way, that recovery is possible.
4. The fact that more can be had for less, that the right way also happens to be the cheaper way. And, in an age of austerity, that has to be a winner.

This time round we can not afford to fail. Consider this: This book is, in a sense, a plea from the coal face to the pit-head office. Here we are in Balsall Heath and many other neighbourhoods hacking away at the coal face of renewal. But, we are trapped, can't get out, can't move to another area, have too few tools to escape or deliver our truck load of goods to the surface.

Every previous top-down pit-head attempt to reach us has been an expensive failure. This time we are shouting back: "Don't give us what you and your officials think we want. We'll tell you what we need. It starts with those Community Organisers, goes on to include Neighbourhood Managers and ends up with devolved Neighbourhood Budgets and investing in us to save you money. We've waited down here for long enough. Don't dither. Do it."

Will key players in Whitehall and the Town Hall hear this plea for action and act on it? No matter how well intentioned the political leader may be, no matter how fine their words and policies are, the Government's response to our plea will fail unless it is driven forward with absolute determination and resolve. To muster the resolve, those concerned must consider that the ending of the social recession and improving the quality of life in 3,000 neighbourhoods is at stake and that millions of residents are depending on them. Indeed, the quality and nature of the whole society is dependent upon them.

The signs are hopeful. The Social Justice Commission set up by Iain Duncan Smith has done and is doing excellent work. Liam Byrne MP who is Iain's shadow secretary for work and pensions called for a re-evaluation of the Welfare State in January 2012. The process of adjusting old forms and old attitudes can not go on for ever. The new thinking of Iain, Liam and which comes from the new planning and budgeting pilots will eventually result in new forms and new attitudes prevailing. The sooner the better from the point of view of all the Teds, Rajas and Naseems out there in so many neighbourhoods.

Chapter 12

CONCLUSION

It is, perhaps, understandable that at times of economic plenty people felt able to throw extra money at neighbourhoods to try to solve the problem of the social recession. They did not feel any pressure to use existing money differently or more effectively. So, they could avoid the hard, but essential task of working out how to change the way services were delivered to residents in neighbourhoods. So, the lessons from Balsall Heath could be ignored.

Now that times are financially more constrained there is an extra reason for pausing and applying these lessons. If it really is possible to get 'more for less' then all concerned should sit up and take notice. Indeed, once safely ignored, Balsall Heath is now one of a significant number of Government backed neighbourhood planning and budgeting pilots which has Birmingham City Council's backing. That's significant. Consider this:

Twenty years ago a car was parked in Balsall Heath outside a fast-food take-away shop. The occupants, a man, woman and two children took their take-away into the car and ate it. Then, one by one they wound down their windows and tipped the used cartons and plastic bags into the already litter-strewn gutter.

Naseem was passing. As the car was about to drive off she tapped on the window and politely invited the occupants to pick up their rubbish and put it in a nearby bin or take it home. The woman said: "That's what we have street sweepers for." Naseem persisted. The man joined in, called her an "interfering busy-body" and drove off with the children laughing on the back seat.

A few days later, the meeting described in Chapter 3 was held between residents, the Council and the Police in which the residents asked for prostitution and kerb crawling to be ended, the litter to be cleared and Balsall Heath's quality of life to be improved. The reader will recall that those in authority replied: "Sorry, we can't. We're doing all we can. If you don't like it, move." Perhaps it's time to add that as the officials left the meeting, the senior environmental service officer whispered to Naseem: "If you lot didn't put down the rubbish faster than my team can pick it up, maybe we could do our job." Naseem blushed and resolved to somehow do something.

We are in the middle of a social recession. It has been deepening for several decades. It has grown, in part, because the well intentioned Welfare State did things 'to' and 'for' people. It fed them fish. It picked up their litter and, along with other factors, made them dependent and careless of each other. It atomised the village which children need to guide and educate them. To date, politicians have failed to find a fresh way forward.

It took Naseem, Raja and ordinary residents who were desperate to provide their children with a healthy neighbourhood in which to grow up to see a way forward. They taught each other to care and to fish for themselves.

They became independent and proud and showed us all how to re-order the Welfare State and end the social recession. Balsall Heath now wins plaudits in the annual Britain in Bloom competition. Raja's Trades Union experience enabled him and others to reclaim the streets from criminals. At last, the environmental officer and the Police are able to do their job. Indeed, that job is now a different, more effective one. It just so happens that building social capital and ending the social recession by enabling people to fish for themselves is also financially far cheaper than being provided with fish. So, it also contributes to the easing of the economic recession and, for the first time, makes neighbourhood renewal sustainable.

However, ending the social recession entails dramatic changes not just in the way residents behave but in the way the Welfare State in structured. Until recently it was by no means certain that the optimistic vision painted by Balsall Heath and a few other areas would be realised in many neighbourhoods. So, two stark alternatives face us over the coming years.

1. In one neighbourhood a small group of teenagers and young men in their twenties live in 2 adjacent streets. They are out of work and draw benefits. But, they don't look for jobs. Rather, they band together, regularly assault passers by, steal their purses and mobile phones. This makes their neighbours feel insecure and anxious about going out in the day, let alone in the evening.

    Recently, they have moved into the world of scrap metal trading. They travel to nearby churches and railway lines, take the lead off roofs and copper cables and, thus, supplement their benefits and cause a great deal of both social pain and costly repairs.

    A glance at the Council Houses they live in reveals curtains drawn in the afternoon, overgrown and untended gardens. The alleyways between the houses are unusable because they are filled with litter, rubber from cables and weeds. The image of their neighbourhood is poor. Businesses struggle to survive.

Two of the young men were arrested and tried in court because of their involvement in the riots of August 2011. They were recently imprisoned for four years at a cost of £50k each per year. They and their friends do not feel very content. Nor are they very well. Their life expectancy is much lower than the national average.

Not only do they cost the Welfare State and taxpayer huge amounts in benefits, the cost of crimes and imprisonment, they also inadvertently cause their whole neighbourhood to be unproductive and untrusting.

There is no Forum for the neighbourhood and also residents don't socialise very much. They stay at home or hurry to the shops and back again. Many old people are put into institutional care because there is nobody in the community to look after them. There is no liaison between the fractured community and Statutory Players who deliver the services they think people need.

The Neighbourhood costs a very great deal of money, but puts very little of that money back into the communal pot and nobody in the neighbourhood feels that they can influence the way that money is spent. Just 20% of the population vote in Council elections.

2. A similarly aged group of young people in an adjacent neighbourhood were helped by their well led school and parents to be ambitious. Some are in further training. Others have jobs. They all belong to their local youth centre and play organised games where there is a very good youth organiser. He has persuaded the group to volunteer to visit lone elderly people in their area, run errands for them and do minor repairs.

    In addition, they tend the Council House gardens of those elderly folk so that they can sit out in them in the Spring, Summer and Autumn months and chat to their passing neighbours. The youngsters don't see this as a chore. They enjoy doing it and gain the sense of pride and personal wealth.

    Moreover, in part because they live happy and gainful lives they also live longer, close to the national average. Their neighbourhood thrives as do local businesses.

    Many residents enjoy meeting together in the local school where they organise entertainment and the occasional communal meal.

They have formed a Neighbourhood Forum whose members attend the local Ward Committee and liaise with the police and council in what they call a Neighbourhood Hub. There is a Neighbourhood Strategic Partnership. It has written a Neighbourhood Plan, agreed and distributed a Neighbourhood Budget. So, their Statutory Partners are able to adjust their services to suit the local need. The vote in local elections has risen and reached 44%.

At a recent committee meeting in the Council House, one of the Councillors who represents the Ward in which neighbourhood 1 falls urged that some money be set aside to repair some broken windows in the local library. He was told that no money was available.

The 3 Councillors who represent neighbourhood 2 recently attended a weekend gathering of volunteers who were taming the overgrown, unusable, garden of a small block of Council flats in which several elderly people lived. Once the job was done the elderly people brought out cups of tea for all concerned and thanked them. One of the Councillors turned to the organiser of the volunteers and said: "My term of office ends in May. Why don't you stand in my place?" The organiser said: "But, I'm not a political person." The answer was: "So what, you get things done. People trust you."

Residents in example number 1 cost a lot and undermine a lot. Residents in example number 2 cost far less and save far more. They also build their neighbourhood up. They help other residents to enjoy living in it.

These 2 examples are stark contrasts. The former is the unintended product of the Welfare State and of Beveridge Mark I. The later is the harbinger of the Welfare Society and of Beveridge Mark II.

Of course, life is never quite so black and white as these examples. Many neighbourhoods contain a mixture of the 2 and blur our perception of them and the prescriptions we make for improving the way our society works. So, we need to separate out and identify the 2 trends, the expensive damage caused by the former and the cost effective benefits which flow from the latter. Then we must ask:

- How do we diminish and constrain the former?
- And, how do we support and boost the latter?

Answering these questions has been the aim of this book. How can we summarise the answers we have given?

Neighbourhood 1 is the inadvertent, unintended and very expensive result of the well intentioned Welfare State and of centralised collectivism which eradicates individualism and personal care.

Almost all attempts to correct its deficiencies by top-down renewal initiatives have also been very expensive failures. As a result, there are many more neighbourhoods today which are like number 1 than there were 40 years ago. Indeed, there are at least 3,000 of them.

This is because we have failed to use the talents and energies of ordinary people, they have been an underutilised asset, the passive customer of top-down services, which have provided fish but which merely resulted in the provision of more fish tomorrow and the creation of a dependent population. Neighbourhood 1, the Welfare State which catered for it and conventional left/right politics have run their course.

Neighbourhood 2 empowers residents. It puts them in the driving seat of renewal, enables them to fish for themselves, to be the active and choosy customers of top-down services which, as a result, have to be transformed so that they and the budgets which fund them become neighbourhood specific.

As a consequence we don't just need Active Residents, but also a series of local programmes of action and a national one which calls for:

1. A Resident Organiser and:
   * A Residents Forum
   * A Neighbourhood Hall and Two Men and a Van.

2. A Neighbourhood Strategic Partnership between residents and their Statutory Partners and:
   * A Neighbourhood Manager.
   * A Neighbourhood Plan.
   * A Neighbourhood Budget and other assets transferred to local management.

3. A Residents Academy supported by the local University.

4. A new style of Councillor and MP and
   * A new type of Government Department.
   * A series of rolling programmes of renewal which gradually takes in all 3,000 troubled neighbourhoods.

5. A new culture of care and moral authority.

If Balsall Heath stood alone we might hesitate in being so certain and confident of the success – and financial savings – that this would bring. But, it does not stand alone. Other examples of success are scattered throughout the land. Castle Vale in Birmingham's outer ring is one such example, Royds in Bradford is another. In addition there are now 120 Neighbourhood Planning pilots and 10 Neighbourhood Budgeting ones. The penny is dropping. The building blocks are in place.

When William Beveridge wrote his famous Report in the 1930's it changed the way we structured society and gave the Welfare State a huge boost. He aimed to abolish these five 'evil giants': Want, Disease, Ignorance, Squalor and Idleness.

Few now 'want' in the way people did then. The National Health Service has enabled us all to live many years longer. There is universal schooling for all and squalor has been all but abolished. But, it has to be said, the system of benefits for those who are out of work encourage many to stay out of work. That is, inadvertently, Beveridge and the Welfare State have actually made idleness and dependence pay. Those who are idle want for little and do not live in squalor. Far too many people are, therefore, happy to live via the benefits they gain from the taxes paid by people who do work. They are passive. They rely on others to give them fish to ease their hunger.

Had Beveridge been alive today he might have underpinned our plea for the Welfare Society with the help of Iain Duncan Smith and Liam Byrne by acknowledging that his attempts to rid society of 'want' and 'squalor' had unintentionally contributed significantly to the growth of 'idleness'. So, this time round he might have deleted 4 of his sins and added "carelessness, isolation, passivity and dependence". In this new century, can we now tackle these new evil blights with the same degree of rigour and passion that we tackled those of the last century?

If so, Government needs to give the fisherman and the miner at the coal face the active support of a radically new Department of State which will significantly change the way Central and Local Government works so that they stop providing fish and enable people to fish for themselves.

This change from the Welfare State to the Welfare Society is as radical as that entailed in setting up the Welfare State itself. But, it also entails changing the role of the Councillor and of the way the political parties operate. If we are to have a new breed of Community Champion, then we need to recruit at least some future Councillors from the ranks of Active Citizens and not just active party members.

Are the parties up for it? Can the State transform itself from within? Can the Active Resident set the agenda for tomorrow and ensure that we end up in a few years with 3,000 transformed neighbourhoods? Time will tell. So also will the vision and wisdom of our political and faith leaders, and the determination and staying power of all those Teds, Rajas and Naseems in all those troubled neighbourhoods. Their dedicated work prevents many expensive-to-solve problems from arising. Prevention really is better and cheaper than cure. It is useful to be reminded of this at a time of financial recession. For, it means we don't need more money. We just need more Naseems.

If we can come together on particular days of national mourning or celebration, surely we can also come together to meet this challenge. Just picture the scenes when Prince William and Kate Middleton married. Or, when Princess Diana's funeral took place. Or, every year on the eleventh hour of the eleventh day of the eleventh month. Imagine the number of people engaged with the celebrations of the Queen's Diamond Jubilee and all those who organised street and other parties. Then ask: "Is it beyond the wit and will of all those people and senior Politicians of all parties to find a way of catering for the renewal of our society?"

If we proceed in this way then, within a generation, we will have achieved what successive Governments failed to achieve over the last 50 years. We will have breathed fresh life not just into the way we care for each other, but also into the whole democratic process. The coal face and the pit-head will at last have a direct and mutually appreciated line of communication. Indeed, they will have just what the Whitehall all party Committee calls for – an agreed programme of action to renew the neighbourhoods of the land. Teaching people to fish really does feed them for life and it makes them proud. It caters for Civil Renewal. And, it's far, far, cheaper than giving them fish.

BIBLIOGRAPHY

Ashdown, Paddy, Beyond Westminster, Simon and Schuster

Atkinson, Dick, Radical Alternative, Orthodox Consensus, Heineman

Atkinson, Dick, Radical Urban Solutions, Heineman

Atkinson, Dick, Cities of Pride, Heineman

Atkinson, Dick, The Common Sense of Community, DEMOS

Atkinson, Dick, Towards Self-governing Schools, IEA

Atkinson, Dick, Urban Renaissance, Brewin Books

Atkinson, Dick, Civil Renewal, Brewin Books

Attwood, Chris, 2001 Home Office Citizenship Survey, Home Office

Baker, Nicola, Building a Relational Society, Arena

Bright, Jon, Turning the Tide, DEMOS

Canterbury, Archbishop of, Faith in the City, Church House

Christine, Ian, An Inclusive Future, DEMOS

Csikszentmihalyi, Mihaly, Living Well, Weidenfeld and Nicolson

Darling, Alastair, The Changing Welfare State, HMSO

Davis, Nick, Dark Heart, Vintage

Elstee, John, Local Justice, Cambridge Press

Etzioni, Amitai, The Spirit of Community, Crown

Field, Frank, Making Welfare Work, Institute of Community Studies

Fordham, Scott, Kemp, Richard, and Crowsley, Paul, Going the extra mile, The JRF

Gidens, Anthony, The Third Way, Polity

Golman, Daniel, Emotional Intelligence, Bloomsbury

Handy, Charles, The Age of Unreason, Hutchinson

Holman, Robert, A New Deal for Social Welfare, Lion

Leadbeater, Charles, The Rise of the Social Entrepreneur, DEMOS
    Leadbeater, Charles and Gross, Sue, Civic Entrepreneur, DEMOS

Leadbeater, Charles, Living on Thin Air, Viking

Mujtaba & Lari, Western Civilisation Through Muslim Eyes, Panjtani Books

Olasky, Marvin, Compassionate Conservation, Free Press

Osborne and Gaebler, Reinventing Government, Addison Wesley and Renguine

Philips, Melanie, All shall have Prizes, Little Brown

Power, Anne & Tunstall, Dangerous Disorder, The Joseph Rowntree Foundation

Power, Anne and Mumford, Katherine, The Slow Death of Great Cities

Power, Anne, Estates of the Edge, Macmillan Press
Power, Anne, One Size does not fit All, BCC
Putnam, Robert, Bowling Alone, Simon and Schuster
Rifkin, Jeremy, The End of Work, Tarcher Puntnan
Rodgers, Lord Richard, Towards Urban Renaissance, HMSO
Shumacher, Eric, Small is Beautiful, Penguin
Sacks, Johnathan, Faith in the Future, Darton, Longman & Treld
Sacks, Johnathan, The Politics of Hope, Jonathan Cape
Skidelsky, Robert, Beyond the Welfare State, Social Market Foundation
Stewart, Valarie, The David Solution, Gower
Taylor, Marilyn, Top Down meets Bottom Up, The Joseph Rowntree Foundation
Taylor, Marilyn, Unleashing the Potential, The Joseph Rowntree Foundation
Thake, Stephen, Staying the course
Thake, Stephen, Practical People, Noble Causes, The JRF
Van der Eyben, Williams, Home-start, Home-start consultancy
Wadhams, Chris, Thursday's Children, The Quest Trust
Wales, The Prince of, A Vision of Britain, Doubleday
Wann, Mai, Building Social Capital, IPPR
Willets, David, Civic Conservatism, The Social Market Foundation
Willets, David, Modern Conservatism, Penguin Books
Wilson, James Q, The Moral Sense, Free Press
Whelan, Robert, Involuntary Action, IEA
Whelan, Robert, Octavia Hill, IEA

BY THE SAME AUTHOR

Radical Alternative, Orthodox Consensus, Heineman
Radical Urban Solutions, Heineman
Cities of Pride, Heineman
The Common Sense of Community, DEMOS
Towards Self-governing Schools, IEA
Urban Renaissance, Brewin Books
Civil Renewal, Brewin Books